The American West

ROSEMARY REES

General Editor: Josh Brooman

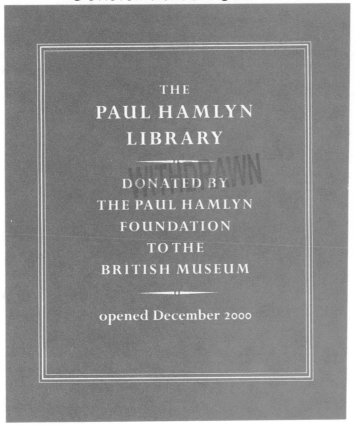

 LONGMAN

Addison Wesley Longman Limited

Edinburgh Gate, Harlow, Essex. CM20 2JE England.

© Addison Wesley Longman Limited 1996

First published 1996
Third Impression 1997

ISBN 0 582 289491

The right of Rosemary A. Rees to be identified as author of this work has been asserted by her in accordance with the Copyright, Designs and Patents Act 1988.

Printed in Great Britain by Scotprint Limited, Musselburgh, Scotland.

Design and production by Hart McLeod, Cambridge. Set in Concorde and Tecton

Illustrations by Sheila Betts

The Publisher's policy is to use paper manufactured from sustainable forests.

Cover: Peter Newark's Western Americana

Acknowledgements

We are grateful to the following for permission to reproduce photographs.

American Heritage Center, University of Wyoming, pages 10, 94; Location unknown/Bridgeman Art Library, London, page 13, National Museum of American Art, Smithsonian Inst./Bridgeman, pages 14, 33; British Library Newspaper Library, page 77; British Museum (Museum of Mankind), page 22 (left); taken from *The Century Magazine*, page 27, *The Century Magazine*, Volume 41, Nov. 1890, page 37; the Denver Public Library, Western History Department, page 49; Mary Evans Picture Library, pages 6, 52 (below);Werner Forman Archive/Museum fur Volkerkunde, Berlin, page 22 (right), 28 (below right), WFA/C. Porht Collection, Plains Indians Museum, B. Hill History Centre, Cody, Wyoming, page 25 (below), WFA, page 28 (above right); N.C. Wyeth, 'The James Brothers': Not dated, oil on canvas, 25" x 40", (acc. no. 0127, 1544), 'From the Collection of Gilcrease Museum, Tulsa' page 91 (right), C Schreyvogel, 'Attack at Dawn': Dated 1904, oil on canvas, 34" x 46", (acc. no. 0127.1255), 'From the Collection of Gilcrease Museum, Tulsa', page 108 (below); Glasgow Museums: Art Gallery and Museum, Kelvingrove, page 122; The Ronald Grant Archive, page 70; taken from *Harpers Monthly*, page 21; Hulton Deutsch Collection, pages 25 (above), 52 (above); Missouri Historical Society, St Louis, page 119; Solomon D Butcher. Collection/Nebraska State Historical Society, pages 78, 80, 85; Peter Newark's Western Americana, pages 12, 17, 18, 24, 28 (above left), 29, 30, 50, 55, 56, 59, 60, 62, 64 (left), 64 (right), 66, 68, 69, 71, 76, 82, 83, 90, 91 (left), 93, 102, 108 (above), 109, 112, 120; The New-York Historial Society, page 40; Oklahoma Historical Society, page 11; Range/Bettmann, page 45; Smithsonian Institution, page 19, (neg. no. 75-4268), page 113, (neg. no. 55-299), page 117, (neg. no. 55-018); Courtesy of the Southwest Museum, Los Angeles, (photo 1026.G.1).

Picture Research by Sandie Huskinson-Rolfe (PHOTOSEEKERS).

The written sources in this book are taken from many different kinds of published material. Some were originally written in old-fashioned or unusual language. In most cases, unusual or difficult words are explained in the margin. In the rare cases where this has not been possible the wording has been slightly adapted. In many of the sources words have been left out. A cut in the middle of a sentence is shown like this ...; and at the end of a sentence like this ....

Contents

Unit 1 · Introduction

The story of America and the American West is the story of a frontier being pushed west by the grim determination of ordinary men and women. It is an exciting story of courage and bravery, despair and failure, hard work and prosperity, and treachery and greed.

What is a frontier?

Frontiers on earth divide and separate people and land. Only in the twentieth century has the whole world been charted and known. Before this, land frontiers divided the known and settled lands from the unknown and unsettled lands. Sometimes natural frontiers would be obvious – a range of mountains, a river or a desert. Sometimes the frontier would be a line drawn on a map by a government, a queen or an emperor. Some frontiers were permanent, agreed between the owners or rulers of known land. Others were not permanent, and were pushed further and further out as men and women explored and settled land which previously had been unknown.

You can see from the map in Source 1 that America's natural frontiers made it difficult, in the eighteenth and nineteenth centuries, for people to

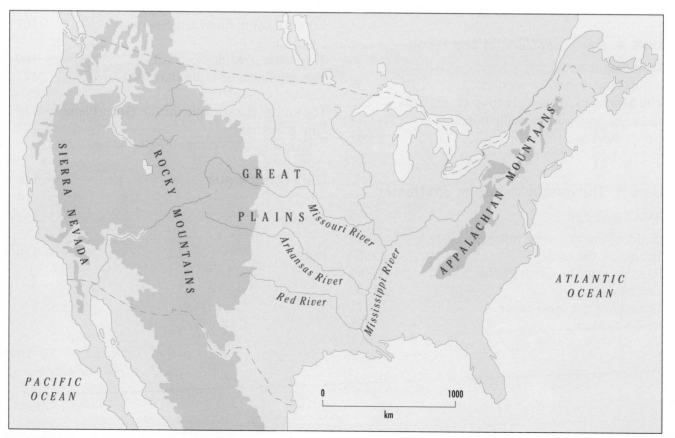

push westwards across the continent. Men and women would only try to cross these natural barriers when they became desperate. They would only struggle over mountains, rivers and plains when their need to leave the places which they knew was greater than their fear of the unknown.

The Appalachian Mountains were 2,000 m high, with steep rock faces and deep valleys. They kept the first white settlers on the eastern coast of the continent. The Mississippi River, wide, slow and treacherous, formed the next natural frontier. Beyond the Mississippi came the prairie grasslands and the Great Plains. Dry, arid, with sudden storms, scorching sun and droughts, the Great Plains were quite a different frontier. They stretched for hundreds of kilometres to the foothills of the Rocky Mountains and the Sierra Nevada. These mountain chains were over 1,000 km wide and over 5 km high, with deep ravines and high passes that were completely blocked by snow for months every winter. They were the final natural frontier standing in the way of people moving westwards.

Lines on the map

People themselves made frontiers. In 1783 the 13 states shown on the map in Source 2 were all that there was of the United States of America. Ten years earlier these states had been colonies belonging to Great Britain. Between 1776 and 1783 the colonies fought Great Britain and won their independence from British rule. There was, however, more to America than these 13 states. In the 1790s parts of the rest of the continent were unknown to Europeans. Some parts had been claimed and occupied by the British, the Spanish and the French. Yet by 1848 the American government owned all of present-day America from the Canadian border to Mexico, and from the Atlantic to the Pacific coasts.

How was the frontier pushed westwards?

By 1800 American settlers had pushed the frontier with the west as far as the Mississippi River. Here they stopped. The lands the other side of this natural frontier were owned by France, Britain and Mexico. In 1803 the US government bought the land owned by France for $15 million. In 1804 the President of the USA sent two explorers, Lewis and Clark, to explore this 'Louisiana Purchase' (see Source 3 on page 6). The way westwards was open once more. In 1846 Britain and the USA agreed that the border between British Canada and the USA should be the 49th Parallel. This meant that the USA owned all of Oregon south of the border with Canada. California belonged to Mexico, and the Mexican government had encouraged white Americans to settle there. However, war broke out between Mexico and the United States in 1846. Mexico was forced to surrender, and the USA gained all Mexican lands north of the Rio Grande and Gilas rivers. This included California.

By 1853, through a combination of good luck, force, treaties and money, the USA owned the whole of the land of America from coast to coast and from the Canadian border to Mexico. No one knew, however, whether they would be able to hold on to this land. Would Mexico become strong enough to challenge the American hold on Texas and California? Would France regret the sale of Louisiana? Would Britain try

Source 2

The original 13 states of North America.

New Hampshire

New York

Massachusetts

Rhode Island

Connecticut

Pennsylvania

New Jersey

Delaware

Maryland

Virginia

North Carolina

South Carolina

Georgia

ATLANTIC OCEAN

0   1000

km

Source 3   The growth of North America, 1783–1853.

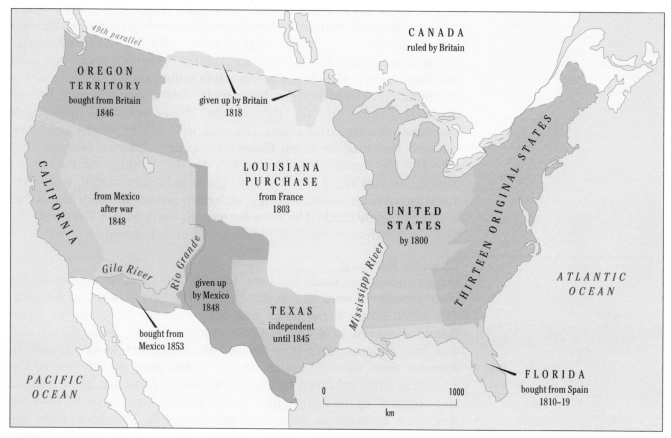

49th parallel

CANADA
ruled by Britain

OREGON TERRITORY
bought from Britain 1846

given up by Britain 1818

CALIFORNIA

from Mexico after war 1848

LOUISIANA PURCHASE
from France 1803

UNITED STATES
by 1800

THIRTEEN ORIGINAL STATES

Gila River

Rio Grande

given up by Mexico 1848

bought from Mexico 1853

TEXAS
independent until 1845

Mississippi River

ATLANTIC OCEAN

PACIFIC OCEAN

0   1000

km

FLORIDA
bought from Spain 1810–19

to alter the Canadian border? As far as the US government was concerned, the only way to hold on to the land was to fill it with loyal, white Americans. The lands beyond the Mississippi, though, were not empty lands. The people who lived there were a people with different hopes, ambitions and beliefs from those of the white Americans. They were the native peoples of America – the North American Indians. The story of the American West, then, is not only about pushing the frontier of settlement westwards. It is also about the dramatic and bitter clash between these two groups – the white people and the North American Indians.

Source 4

A contemporary etching of the Lewis and Clark expedition of 1804. They explored the Louisiana Purchase, crossed the Rocky Mountains and the Sierra Nevada and reached the Pacific coast. Their expedition was the first journey by Europeans overland from the Mississippi westwards to the sea.

Unit 2 · The Plains Indians

The Indians you will read about in this book are the Plains Indians – mainly the Cheyenne, Arapaho, Comanche, Kiowa and Kiowa Apache on the southern Plains, and the Crows and Sioux to the north. They played an important part in the history of the American West. It was the Plains Indians who fiercely resisted the white people in their attempt to push the frontier westward across the Great Plains to the Pacific coast. It was the Plains Indians who had their way of life altered forever by successive waves of white people, cattlemen and cowboys, pioneers and homesteaders, all of whom wanted to use the Great Plains for their own purposes. It was the Plains Indians who stood in the way of white Americans who believed that America was there to make the white people rich and prosperous.

Where did the Plains Indians come from?

Twenty thousand years ago America was not a separate continent as it is today. It was linked to Asia by land which joined present-day Alaska to present-day Siberia. Archaeologists have found the bones of animals that wandered into America from Asia. They have discovered ancient stone fireplaces and arrow heads which were made by people living many thousands of years ago. The archaeologists worked out that people followed these animals down into the continent of America. The animals moved in large herds and were easy to follow and easy to kill. Men, women and children moved down through America, following the animal trails. As a Sioux Indian explains, land was very important to them.

Source 1

White Thunder, a Sioux Indian, quoted in Dee Brown, *Bury My Heart at Wounded Knee*, 1971.

Our land here is the dearest thing on earth to us.

Source 2 on page 8 shows the movement of animals and people between Asia and America. This movement ended when geological shifts in the earth's crust meant that hundreds of square kilometres of solid land finally disappeared underneath the sea and Asia and America were separated. By this time the peoples who Europeans were later to call 'Indians' were firmly established in America. There were many different tribes and nations of Indians living in the rocky mountains, the wooded valleys and the sandy desert fringes (see Source 3). Over thousands of years they adapted their lives to the surroundings in which they lived. The Iroquois in the fertile east, for example, were farmers and fishermen, the Teton Sioux on the plains were hunters, and the Bannock and Ute tribes in the mountain regions lived on berries, roots and grubs.

Source 2
This map shows how the Indians came to North America.

Source 3
This map shows where the main North American Indian tribes lived.

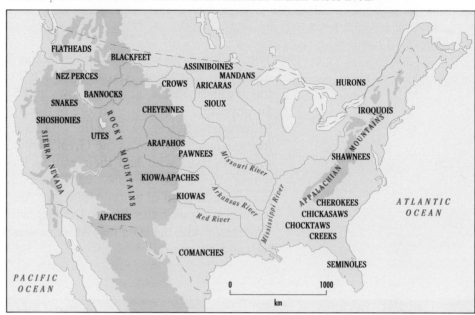

Horses and hunters

For a long time the Plains Indians were poor tribes, living difficult and dangerous lives, often close to starvation. The Great Plains themselves were bare and empty, except for the herds of buffalo which drifted over the vast empty spaces, grazing wherever the grass was sweetest. The Indians lived on the fringes of the Great Plains. They grew maize and beans, and hunted buffalo on foot when they needed meat. What' happened to turn these people into proud chiefs and brave warriors, ready and able to challenge the white Americans who came with their advanced technology, their dreams and their greed? The answer lies in one animal: the horse.

There were no horses in America until about 400 years ago. In the sixteenth century the Spanish conquered the tribes living in Central America and settled there. They built towns and began to farm on a large scale. They bred horses, but always refused to sell any to the Indians. Then, in 1640, the Pueblo Indians rose up against the Spanish. They drove them out and captured their horses. The Pueblo kept some horses for meat and some for breeding. The rest they sold to other Indian tribes. So the Plains Indians came to own horses, and their lives were never the same again. With horses, they could follow the huge herds of buffalo over the Great Plains and hunt them much more efficiently. The Plains Indians need never be hungry again. Their way of life had changed forever. Forever, that is, until the white people came to the Great Plains.

The Plains Indians became marvellous horse-riders, skilled at hunting, fighting and sport. They certainly prized their animals and thought of them as important warriors, as you can see from Source 4. These Sioux war ponies are painted with designs which were just as special as those with which the Indians painted themselves.

Source 4
Sioux ponies decorated for war.

Questions

1 **a** What is an archaeologist?
   b How do archaeologists find out about the past?
   c Why do we need archaeologists to tell us about America's Indians?

2 Why were horses so important to the Plains Indians?

3 Why are the Plains Indians important in the history of the American West?

What were the beliefs of the Plains Indians?

The Great Spirit

All Indians believed in the Great Spirit. The Great Spirit ruled over everything. He lived in the Happy Hunting Ground, a beautiful country beyond the skies. The Indians' greatest hope was to go to the Happy Hunting Ground when they died, and they were only likely to do this if they had served the Great Spirit well during their lifetime.

As well as believing in the one Great Spirit, the Plains Indians believed that all natural things had spirits of their own. This meant that humans, animals, insects, fish, plants and birds all had to be treated with the same sort of respect. There was a closeness between man and all natural things because Indians believed that all life was holy. Man was no more important than any other living creature. Black Elk, a holy man of the Oglala Sioux, expresses it like this:

Source 1
Black Elk in J Neihardt, *Black Elk Speaks*, 1974.

My friend, I am going to tell you the story of my life. It is the story of all that is holy and good to tell, and of us two leggeds sharing it with the four leggeds and the wings of the air – all green things; for these are children of one mother and their father is one spirit.

Circles

Plains Indians were convinced that the power of the earth always moved and worked in circles. Circles were all around them. The sky was round and so was the sun which shone in it. The wind whirled in circles, and the seasons formed one great circle, always coming back to where they started. Birds built their nests in circles, and the Indians themselves had round homes, tipis, which they set up in circles. Even the life of man was a circle, beginning with childhood and ending with very old people behaving like children.

The Indians believed they could use this power of the earth if they understood the natural world properly, and tried to work with it and not against it. This power would then become the Indians' power.

Source 2

A modern photograph of the 'medicine wheel', a circle deliberately built by the Indians, on Medicine Mountain in Wyoming.

Each Indian tribe gave their own special names to the months of the year. These showed the Indians' closeness to all natural things.

Source 3

Black Elk tells the names the Sioux gave to the months of the year. In J Neihardt, *Black Elk Speaks*, 1974.

January:	Moon of the Frost in the Tipi
February:	Moon of the Dark Red Calves
March:	Moon of the Snow Blind
April:	Moon of the Red Grass Appearing
May:	Moon when the Ponies Shed
June:	Moon of Making Fat
July:	Moon of the Red Cherries
August:	Moon when the Cherries turn Black
September:	Moon when the Calves grow Hair
October:	Moon of the Changing Season
November:	Moon of the Falling Leaves
December:	Moon of the Popping Trees

Source 4

Part of a painting on an animal skin showing an Apache girl's puberty ceremony.

Visions

Visions were very important to all Indians. They believed it was through visions that they could come into contact with the spirits and with the one Great Spirit which flows through the universe.

Indians believed that girls could easily make contact with the spirit world. When a girl began her monthly periods she automatically had the power to talk to the spirits. Girls had to be taught how to control the spirits before they controlled her. They were taken away by old women of the tribe and taught what to do. When a girl had learned what to do, she went back to her tribe and her family. She was then given her adult name amid much feasting and rejoicing.

Indian boys had to go looking for their vision. They went to a sweat lodge where they got their bodies ready by making sure they were clean, and their minds ready by going without food and praying. When a young man had had his vision, he went back to his tribe. The medicine man would interpret the vision, the young Indian would be given his adult name, one connected with his vision, and everyone would rejoice. When he was a child, a boy might be called 'No Teeth' or 'Fat Toes'. After his vision he might become 'Grey Raven' or 'Running Water'.

Source 5

Black Elk describes his vision in J. Neihardt, *Black Elk Speaks*, 1974.

This was not a dream. It happened. I was going to shoot a kingbird with the bow my grandfather made, when the bird spoke and said: 'The clouds are all over one-sided.' Perhaps it meant that all the clouds were looking at me. And then it said: 'Listen! A voice is calling you!' Then I looked up at the clouds and two men were coming there, headfirst like arrows slanting down. As they came they sang a sacred song and the thunder was like drumming. The song and the drumming went like this: 'Behold a sacred voice is calling you; all over the sky a sacred voice is calling.' I sat there gazing at them and they were coming from the place where the giant lives. But when they were very close to me they wheeled about to where the sun goes down, and suddenly they were geese. Then they were gone, and the rain came with a big sound and a roaring.

Medicine men

The medicine man, such as the one shown in Source 6, was not only important because he interpreted the visions of young men. He was vital to the life of the tribe. The medicine man could make contact with the

spirits of all living things. Everything he did, from interpreting visions to curing the sick, stemmed from this.

Geronimo, an Apache medicine man, describes some of his work:

> The Indians knew what herbs to use for medicine, how to prepare them and how to give the medicine. This they had been taught in the beginning, and each generation had men who were skilled in the art of healing, in gathering herbs, in preparing them, and in administering the medicine. As much faith was held in prayer as in the actual effect of the medicine.

Source 7 S. M. Barrett (ed.), *Geronimo: His Own Story*, 1974.

Source 6

This picture of a Mandan medicine man, dressed for a Dog Dance, was painted by Karl Bodmer.

Source 8

G. Catlin, *Manners, Customs and Conditions of North American Indians*, 1844.

The medicine man should really be called the 'mystery man' because he was the tribe's most important link with the spirit world. George Catlin, an American artist who travelled amongst the Plains Indians in the 1830s, explains the connection between 'medicine' and 'mystery':

> Medicine is a great word in this country. It is very necessary that one should know the meaning of it. The word medicine means mystery and nothing else.

Each male Indian had his own medicine or 'mystery'. This he kept in a small bag which he wore around his neck. The little bag contained sacred objects – a bird's claw or a flower, perhaps – which had special importance to that particular Indian. He told no one what was in his bag, and when he died it was buried with him. Girls and squaws did not need a medicine bag. They had all the power they needed because they could so easily make contact with the spirit world.

The medicine man was consulted by the chiefs and the Council before war was declared, before peace was made, before the tribe moved hunting grounds, before, in fact, they decided anything important.

Source 9

This picture of a Mandan Buffalo Dance was painted by George Catlin in the 1830s.

Dances

Medicine men could always make contact with the spirits, and, at times, so could individual Indians. Sometimes there was great trouble, when, for example, the huge buffalo herds could not be found. Then the tribe as a whole needed to make contact with the spirits. They did this through many ceremonies and rituals, and especially dances. In all these the medicine men took a leading part.

For the Arapahos and the Cheyennes, the most important ceremony of the year was the Sun Dance. In this dance, an Indian tortured himself to show the tribe his bravery, and bring visions to himself and to the other dancers. Through these visions the dancers hoped to make contact with the spirit world. They hoped to work with the spirits to make themselves better hunters or warriors, and so bring glory to the tribe.

Source 10

Black Elk describes a Sun Dance in J. Neihardt, *Black Elk Speaks*, 1974.

The next day the dancing began, and those who were going to take part were ready, for they had been fasting and purifying themselves in the sweat lodges, and praying. First, their bodies were painted by the holy men. Then each would lay down beneath the tree as though he were dead, and the holy man would cut a place in his back or chest, so that a strip of rawhide, fastened to the top of the tree, could be pushed through the flesh and tied. Then the man would get up and dance to the drums, leaning on the rawhide strip as long as he could stand the pain or until the flesh tore.

Questions

1 What do Sources 1–3 tell you about the feeling that Indians had for the land and all living things?

2 **a** Why were visions important to Indian boys?
b Why did Indian girls not need to look for visions?
c Does the fact that Indian boys had visions, and Indian girls did not, make the girls inferior to the boys?

3 Read Sources 7 and 8. They seem to be saying different things about the meaning of 'medicine'. How do you account for this?

4 Plains Indians were skilled in tracking and hunting buffalo. Why would they spend time taking part in a Buffalo Dance when they could be tracking down the missing buffalo herds?

How important were buffalo to the Plains Indians?

Life was not easy for the Plains Indians. They travelled long distances in freezing winters and scorching summers. Even so, their free and roaming way of life was deeply important to them. Everything in their lives came from the fact that they were nomadic: they did not live in settled communities. They wandered across the Great Plains, setting up camp wherever they happened to stop as they followed the great herds of buffalo on which their lives depended.

Hunting the buffalo

As soon as they had horses, the Plains Indians did not have to stalk buffalo on foot, covered in animal skins to disguise their human smell. They still, from time to time, chased a herd toward a cliff, where the buffalo tumbled to their deaths. But this was just for fun. Nothing could match the excitement of hunting the buffalo on horseback in a thrilling and skilful chase.

Source 1

G. Grinnell, *When the Buffalo Ran*, 1920.

Like an arrow from a bow each horse darted forward. What had been only a wild gallop became a mad race. Each rider hoped to be the first to reach the top of the opposite ridge and to turn the buffalo back into the valley. How swift those little ponies were, and how admirably the Indians managed to get out of them all their speed! I had not gone more than half way across the valley when I saw the leading Indians pass the head of the herd and begin to turn the buffalo. Back came the herd, and I soon found myself in the midst of a throng of buffalo, horses and Indians. There was no yelling or shouting on the part of the men, but their stern, set faces, and the fierce gleam of their eyes, told of the fires of excitement that were burning within them.

Source 2

This buffalo chase was painted by George Catlin in the 1830s.

Source 3

Black Elk in J Neihardt, *Black Elk Speaks*, 1974.

* **bison** Buffalo.

Then the crier shouted like singing: 'Your knives shall be sharpened. Make ready, make haste; your horses make ready! We shall go forth with arrows. Plenty of meat we shall make!' Everybody began sharpening knives and arrows and getting the best horses ready for the great making of meat. Then we started for where the bison* were.

The uses of the buffalo

When the hunters brought the buffalo back to camp, the women cut out the parts that were good to eat raw, like the kidneys, the liver and the brain. The flesh was boiled or roasted. Anything left over was sliced into thin strips and smoked or dried in the sun. This 'jerky', as it was called, would keep for a long time and would help feed the tribe during the cold winter months. The women also made pemmican from leftover meat. They pounded the meat into pulp, mixed it with berries and put it into skin containers. Then they poured hot grease and marrowfat over the containers to make them airtight. Pemmican made like this kept for a long time. Below are two descriptions, one by a white man and one by an Indian, of what happened after a buffalo hunt.

Source 4

Black Elk in J. Neihardt, *Black Elk Speaks*, 1974.

When the butchering was all over, they hung the meat across the horses' backs and fastened it with strips of fresh bison hide. On the way back to the village all the hunting horses were loaded, and we little boys who could not wait for the feast helped ourselves to all the raw liver we wanted. Nobody got cross when we did this.

During this time, women back at the camp were cutting long poles and forked sticks to make drying racks for the meat. When the hunters got home they threw their meat in piles on the leaves of trees. The women were all busy cutting the red meat into strips and hanging it on the racks to dry. You could see the red meat hanging everywhere. The people feasted all night long and danced and sang. Those were happy times.

Source 5

Francis Parkman, *The Oregon Trail*, 1968.

* **squaws** Indian women.
* **lodge** Tipi.

The squaws* flung down the load from the burdened horses, and vast piles of meat and hides were soon gathered before every lodge*. By this time it was darkening fast, and the whole village was illuminated by the glare of fires. All the squaws and children were gathered about the piles of meat, exploring them in search of the daintiest portions. Some of these they roasted on stocks before the fires, but they often dispensed with this operation. Late into the night the fires were still glowing upon the groups of feasters engaged in this savage banquet around them.

The Plains Indians used every part of the buffalo, as Source 6 on page 16 shows. Even the buffalo's tongue was used as a hairbrush, and the dung as fuel! But there was one part of the buffalo which was never used. This was the heart. This did not mean that it was not important. It was cut from the dead animal and left on the Plains to give new life to the herd which had given the Indians the buffalo which they needed so much.

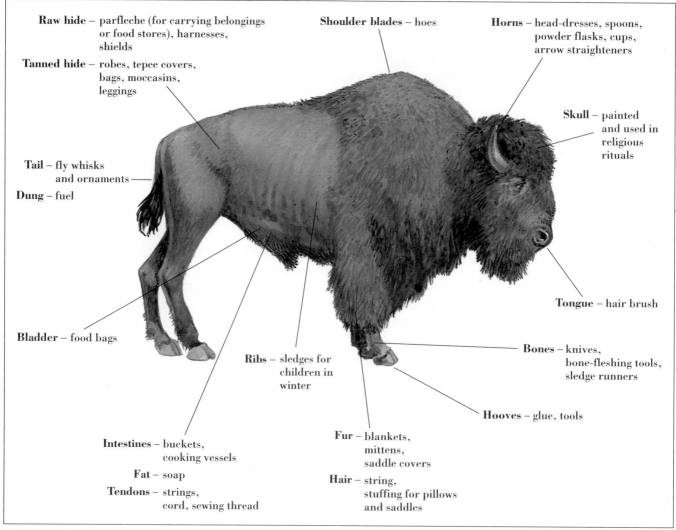

Raw hide – parfleche (for carrying belongings or food stores), harnesses, shields

Tanned hide – robes, tepee covers, bags, moccasins, leggings

Tail – fly whisks and ornaments

Dung – fuel

Bladder – food bags

Intestines – buckets, cooking vessels

Fat – soap

Tendons – strings, cord, sewing thread

Ribs – sledges for children in winter

Fur – blankets, mittens, saddle covers

Hair – string, stuffing for pillows and saddles

Shoulder blades – hoes

Horns – head-dresses, spoons, powder flasks, cups, arrow straighteners

Skull – painted and used in religious rituals

Tongue – hair brush

Bones – knives, bone-fleshing tools, sledge runners

Hooves – glue, tools

Source 6

All the different ways in which Indians used the buffalo.

Questions

1   Which was the more important to the Plains Indians: horses or buffalo?

2   Black Elk (Source 4) and Francis Parkman (Source 5) both describe what happened after a buffalo hunt.
   a On what points do the sources agree?
   b On what points do the sources disagree?
   c Both Francis Parkman and Black Elk are describing what they saw. How can the differences in their accounts be explained?

3   Francis Parkman said 'When the buffalo are extinct, the Indian too must dwindle away'. Do you agree with him? Explain your answer.

What was Indian family life like?

The tipi

The tipi, sometimes called a lodge, was the home of each Indian family. It was a tent with a frame of wooden poles arranged in a circle and covered with between ten and twenty buffalo hides, sewn together. In winter a fire in the middle of the tipi helped keep the family warm and cook their food. The smoke from the fire went out of the hole at the top of the tipi. There was a flap which could be adjusted according to the direction of the wind, so that the smoke blew away and not back down into the tipi. The Indians decorated their tipis inside and out with brightly coloured paintings of animals, birds or geometric designs. They put rugs on the floor, and comfortable cushions made of skins and stuffed with a soft filling. Here are two descriptions of the inside of a tipi:

Source 1

Colonel R. I. Dodge, a white man who travelled for many years amongst the Plains Indians, describes a tipi in his book *Hunting Grounds of the Great West*, 1877.

In this small space are often crowded eight or ten persons, possibly of three or four different families. Since the cooking, eating, living and sleeping are all done in the one room, it soon becomes incredibly filthy.

Source 2

Chief Flying Hawk, of the Oglala Sioux, describes a tipi.

The tipi is always clean, warm in winter and cool in summer.

Source 3

This picture of a Comanche village was painted by George Catlin in the 1830s.

Indians on the move

The Plains Indians needed to follow the vast herds of buffalo which roamed the Great Plains. This meant that their tipis were always being taken down and put up again somewhere else. When the Indians moved camp, they had to take everything with them. They used travois to carry all their possessions. Travois were made from two tipi poles, joined at the horses' shoulders. The other ends trailed on the ground. In the middle of the poles the Indians put a frame or a net for carrying their belongings. Charles Russell's painting (Source 5) shows how this was done.

Source 4

G. Catlin, *Manners, Customs and Conditions of North American Indians*, 1844.

The lodges are taken down in a few minutes by the squaws and easily transported to any part of the country where they wish to encamp. They generally move six to eight times in the summer, following the immense herds of buffalo. The manner in which an encampment of Indians strike their tents and transport them is curious. I saw an encampment of Sioux, consisting of six hundred lodges, struck and all things packed and on the move in a very few minutes. The chief sends his runners through the village a few hours before they are to start, announcing his determination to move, and the hour fixed upon. At the time announced, the lodge of the chief is seen flapping in the wind, a part of the poles having been taken out from under it; this is the signal, and in one minute six hundred of them were flat upon the ground.

Source 5

This painting of Sioux Indians moving camp and using travois was painted at the time by Charles M. Russell.

Henry Boller, who lived among the Plains Indians for some years in the middle of the nineteenth century, wrote a book about his experiences in which he describes an Indian family on the move (Source 6). At the end of the nineteenth century, Indians were still using travois to move their belongings, as you can see in Source 7.

Source 6

H. A. Boller, *Among the Indians: Eight Years in the Far West*, 1972.

About a foot behind the horse, a kind of basket is suspended between the poles and firmly lashed in its place. On the back of the horse are piled various articles of luggage; the basket is also filled with domestic utensils, or, quite as often, with a litter of puppies, a brood of small children, or an old man. Numbers of these curious vehicles (travois) were now splashing together through the stream. Among them swam countless dogs, often burdened with miniature travois themselves. Dashing forward on horseback through the throng came the warriors, the slender figure of some lynx-eyed boy clinging fast behind them. The women sat perched on the pack-saddles, adding not a little to the load of the already overburdened horses. The confusion was tremendous. The dogs yelled and howled in chorus; the puppies in the travois set up a dismal whine as the water invaded their comfortable retreat; the little black-eyed children, from one year of age upward, clung fast with both hands to the edge of their basket.

Source 7

This photograph of Gros Ventre women moving camp with their travois was taken towards the end of the nineteenth century.

Bands, tribes and nations

Indian families, as you have seen, lived together in tipis. Families who were related to each other pitched their tipis together and travelled together in a group called a band. The different bands in a tribe met together for a great tribal summer feast when the grass was rich and sweet enough for all the buffalo they needed. Some tribes were part of a larger group called a nation. The Oglala Sioux and the Teton Sioux, for example, were all part of the Sioux nation.

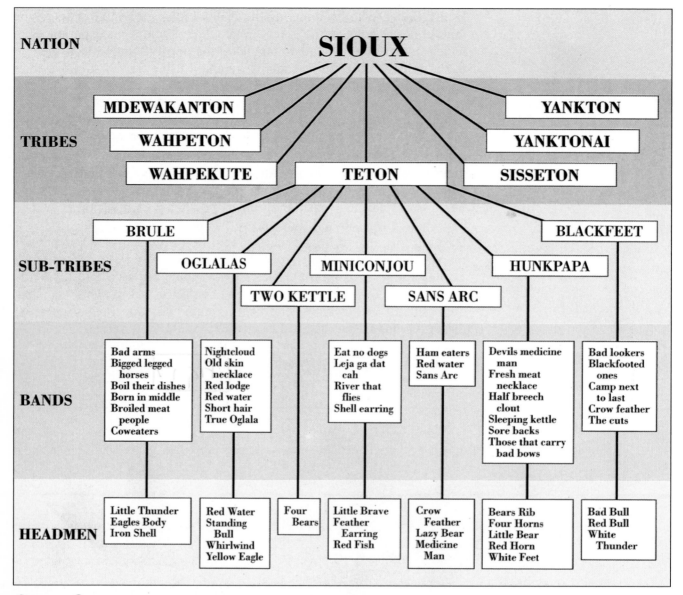

The Sioux nation diagram:

NATION: SIOUX

TRIBES: MDEWAKANTON, WAHPETON, WAHPEKUTE, TETON, YANKTON, YANKTONAI, SISSETON

SUB-TRIBES: BRULE, OGLALAS, TWO KETTLE, MINICONJOU, SANS ARC, HUNKPAPA, BLACKFEET

BANDS:
- Bad arms, Bigged legged horses, Boil their dishes, Born in middle, Broiled meat people, Coweaters
- Nightcloud, Old skin necklace, Red lodge, Red water, Short hair, True Oglala
- Eat no dogs, Leja ga dat cah, River that flies, Shell earring
- Ham eaters, Red water, Sans Arc
- Devils medicine man, Fresh meat necklace, Half breech clout, Sleeping kettle, Sore backs, Those that carry bad bows
- Bad lookers, Blackfooted ones, Camp next to last, Crow feather, The cuts

HEADMEN:
- Little Thunder, Eagles Body, Iron Shell
- Red Water, Standing Bull, Whirlwind, Yellow Eagle
- Four Bears
- Little Brave, Feather Earring, Red Fish
- Crow Feather, Lazy Bear, Medicine Man
- Bears Rib, Four Horns, Little Bear, Red Horn, White Feet
- Bad Bull, Red Bull, White Thunder

Source 8
The Sioux nation.

Children

Indians taught their children to respect all living things. The mother earth and everything which lived on her had a dignity and importance of their own. For this reason parents did not ill-treat their children. They taught them, too, to respect older members of the tribe at all times. Francis Parkman, who stayed with Sioux Chief Big Crow and his family, reported that:

Source 9
Francis Parkman, *The Oregon Trail*, 1968.

Both he and his squaw, like most other Indians, were very fond of their children, whom they indulged to excess and never punished, except in extreme cases, when they threw a bowl of cold water over them.

All members of the family were important to each other. Since they lived in a band in which most people were related to each other, children were never without someone to look after them. Aunts and uncles looked after nephews and nieces if their parents died, and cousins were always treated like brothers and sisters. It was the survival of the band that was important. Sometimes Indians seemed to behave in cruel ways in order to make sure their band survived.

Source 10

H. A. Boller, *Among the Indians: Eight Years in the Far West*, 1972.

A squaw with three small children was also left. She carried one on her back and another in her arms, while the eldest trotted along by her side. Some time after, a young Indian who had loitered behind came up and reported that the squaw had just killed the youngest because it was too small to travel.

As children got older, their families prepared them for the different parts they would have to play when they were adults. A boy learned the skills of a warrior – war and horsemanship. A girl learned how to put up and take down a tipi, and how to cut up and prepare buffalo to provide food and clothing for the family.

Braves and squaws

Many tribes believed that the jobs of men and women were equally important. Men defended the band against enemies, whether two- or four-footed. However, once the band was safe, it was the women who made day-to-day living possible. It was the women of the band who put up and took down the tipi, and who had to see that all the family's possessions

Source 11

This woodcut by Frederic Remington shows a young Indian boy learning how to break a pony. Frederic Remington knew a great deal about the West. He first travelled there in 1880. He had an exciting life as a cowboy, a prospector for gold and a traveller. He followed the Oregon and Santa Fé trails, and visited Indian settlements in his travels over the Plains and mountains.

were loaded on to the travois when they moved camp. It was the women who butchered the buffalo and prepared them for use. In many tribes it was common for the men to have more than one wife, a custom which was very practical, as George Catlin and Edward Denig comment:

Source 12

G. Catlin *Manners, Customs and Conditions of North American Indians*, 1844.

* **polygamy** Having more than one wife at the same time.

I visited the tipi of this young medicine man several times, and saw his four little wives seated round the fire, where all were entering very happily on the duties and pleasures of married life. The ages of these young brides were probably all between 12 and 15 years. In this country polygamy* is allowed; and in this tribe where there are two or three times the number of women than there are of men, such an arrangement answers a good purpose; for so many females are taken care of.

Source 13

Adapted from the diary of Edward Denig, an American trader writing in the middle of the nineteenth century.

To support several women, of course, requires greater effort on the part of the man in hunting, but this is more than made up for in their work of dressing skins. This enables the man to buy guns and other means to hunt more easily. When buffalo are plenty, anyone can kill. The rawhide of the animal has no value. It is the work of putting it into the form of a robe or a skin fit for sale or use that makes it valuable. Women therefore are the greatest wealth an Indian possesses next to his horses.

Source 14

A woman's dress, made from two deerskins sewn together.

Not all Indian marriages were happy. Simply by beating a drum and shouting the words 'I throw her away!' a Cheyenne could divorce his wife. The men, however, did not have it all their own way. There were some tribes in which women owned everything – tipi, cooking pots, tools and children. When a man from one of these tribes wanted to divorce his wife he had to leave everything except the clothes he was wearing and go back to his mother's tipi.

These photographs show how skilful Indian women were at making and decorating clothes.

Source 15   An Indian man's beaded jacket.

Widows and old people

Plains Indians depended on the strength of the band to protect them against their enemies. They had to think of the safety and survival of the whole band as well as of individuals within it. When braves were killed out hunting or in war, their widows were shared out and married to the surviving men. In this way all the women were cared for. In this way, too, all women of child-bearing age had as many children as possible.

Old people were a big problem to tribes which were always on the move. They became too ill or too tired or too weak to keep up with their band. Many old Indians took matters into their own hands and went off by themselves to die. Others insisted that the band leave them behind when they moved camp. Below, George Catlin describes what he saw.

Source 16

G. Catlin *Manners, Customs and Conditions of North American Indians,* 1844.

When we were about to start on our way from the village, my attention was directed to a very aged and emaciated man, who was to be left to starve. 'My children', said he 'our nation is poor, and it is necessary that you should all go to the country where you can get meat. My strength is no more, my days are nearly numbered, and I am a burden to my children. I cannot go, and wish to die.'

This cruel custom of exposing their aged people belongs to all the tribes who roam about the prairies, making severe marches, when such old people are totally unable to ride or walk. It often became absolutely necessary in such cases that they should be left; and they always insist on it, as this old man did.

Questions

1 Read Sources 1 and 2.
   a Why do you think they give such different opinions about tipis?
   b Which source do you think is the more reliable?
   c How would you check?

2 Source 4 describes the way in which an Indian camp was taken down. Did the squaws or the Chief play the more important part?

3 Source 5 shows an Indian band on the move. Source 6 describes a band on the move. Is it the same Indian band? Explain your answer.

4 As you can see from Sources 5, 6 and 7, travelling does not seem to be very comfortable for the Indians! Why, then, did they travel over the Great Plains at all – and in this particular way?

5 Does Source 10 undermine what Source 9 says about Indians caring for their children?

6 Using the sources and information in this section, explain why Indian men were allowed by their tribe to have more than one wife.

7 Were the Indians cruel to their old people?

How did the Indians keep law and order?

Indians did not generally need to keep law and order. Everything was controlled by custom and tradition. Indians hated to do wrong because if they did, they would be badly thought of and publicly shamed. It was not until white people came to the Indian lands that the Indians needed the word 'law'.

The Council

Source 1

A Sioux Council, painted by George Catlin in 1847.

The little government that was needed by Indian tribes was in the hands of a Council of leading men from each band. These men were usually peace chiefs. (Some tribes had different chiefs for war and peace.) Chiefs did not order. They offered advice. The voice of a chief would not necessarily be listened to any more than that of any other respected member of his tribe.

Source 2

E. Wallace and E. A. Hoebel, *The Comanches*, 1954.

When the Comanche were asked 'How did you select your headmen?', answers were vague. As one man put it, 'No one made him such; he just got that way'.

No decision could be made until every man at the Council had agreed to it. It was during Council meetings that the ceremonial smoking of a pipe took place. The Indians believed that the smoke from the pipe would carry their words and their desires up into the spirit world so that the spirits could help the members of the Council make wise decisions.

Source 3

Black Elk in J. Neihardt, *Black Elk Speaks*, 1974.

Because no good thing can be done by man alone, I will first make an offering and send a voice to the Spirit of the World, that it may help me to be true. See, I fill this sacred pipe with the bark of red willow. These four ribbons hanging here on the stem are the four quarters of the universe. The black one is for the west where the thunder beings live to send us rain; the white one for the north, from whence comes the great white cleansing wind; the red one for the east, whence springs the light and where the morning star lives to give men wisdom; the yellow for the south, whence comes the summer and the power to grow. And because it means all this, and more than any man can understand, the pipe is holy.

Source 4

Sioux legend.

All these peoples and all these things of the universe are joined to you who smoke the pipe – all send their voices to Waken Tanka, the Great Spirit. When you pray with this pipe you pray for and with everything.

Source 5

This photograph of an Indian Council was taken in 1891.

Source 6

A pipe of peace. This pipe belonged to the Crow Indians.

Warrior societies

Each tribe had its own warrior societies, and every man belonged to one. Each warrior society had its own special costumes and dances and songs. Members met to talk and exchange ideas. The Blackfoot, and some other tribes, had societies that were graded by age, so that the men moved from one to another as they grew older.

One of the most famous societies was that of the Dog Soldiers of the Cheyenne. Their job was to protect the women and children of the tribe. Because of this it was the Dog Soldiers who gave the orders for all marches to begin. They had, too, to protect the buffalo. They had to make sure that only just enough buffalo were killed for the tribe's needs and that the herd was not disturbed when some buffalo were killed. This was important as the whole herd might have panicked, stampeded and disappeared.

Source 7

Colonel R. I. Dodge, *Hunting Grounds of the Great West*, 1877.

Whatever the power of the Chief and the Council, there is another power to which both have to yield. This is the power of the hunters of the tribe, who form a sort of guild. Among the Cheyennes these men are called 'Dog Soldiers'.

Source 8

Colonel Dodge, *Hunting Grounds of the Great West*, 1877.

I cannot say exactly how the powers and duties of these governmental forms, i.e. chiefs, councils and dog-soldiers blend together. I have never met an Indian or white man who could satisfactorily explain them. The result, however, is fairly good and seems well suited to the character, necessities and peculiarities of the Plains Indians.

Questions

1 Look carefully at the painting by George Catlin (Source 1) and the photograph (Source 5).
   a What conclusions can be drawn about Indian Councils from these pictures?
   b How accurate would you judge these conclusions to be?

2 Read Sources 3 and 4. Why did the Indians rely on the spirits and not their own knowledge, experience and judgement when they had to make decisions?

3 Look back to Source 6 on page 15. How does this source help explain why the power of the Chief and Council had to give way, sometimes, to the power of the warrior societies such as the Dog Soldiers?

How did the Plains Indians fight?

Every young Indian boy dreamed of winning glory in battle. This was, for him, the only way to earn respect. No man could become a chief until he had a record of bravery and success in war.

Source 1
Sioux love song.

You may go on the war-path.
When your name I hear,
Having done something brave
Then I will marry you.

Indians did not go to war to conquer others or to gain territory. They did not want to conquer others or gain land. Indians did not believe anyone could own land, anyway. They did not want to conquer and rule over other tribes, and so they did not have to defend their own tribe against others who wanted to kill and conquer them. Indian warfare was made up of short raids, made by small group, in order to capture horses or to kill men for revenge or honour.

Horses

An Indian band's wealth was counted in the number of horses it owned or had stolen from other tribes. Horse stealing became a great art amongst Indians. The Comanches became particularly artful horse thieves. Young boys learned from an early age how to fight in war and how to handle horses. By the time they were adult warriors, most Indians had learned to be amazingly skilful with horses.

Source 2

This 1890 engraving by Frederic Remington shows a Comanche boy performing a trick on horseback. Such a trick is described in Source 3 on page 28.

Source 3

G. Catlin *Manners, Customs and Conditions of North American Indians*, 1844.

Amongst their feats of riding, there is one which has astonished me more than anything of the kind that I have ever seen, or expect to see, in my life. Every young man in the tribe is able to drop his body upon the side of his horse at the instant he is passing, effectually screened from his enemies' weapons as he lies in an horizontal position behind the body of his horse, with his heel hanging over the horse's back, by which he had the power of throwing himself up again, and changing to the other side of the horse if necessary. In this wonderful condition, he will hang whilst his horse is at the fullest speed, carrying with him his bow and his shield, and also his long lance of fourteen feet in length.

Source 4

Traditional weapons of the Plains Indians.

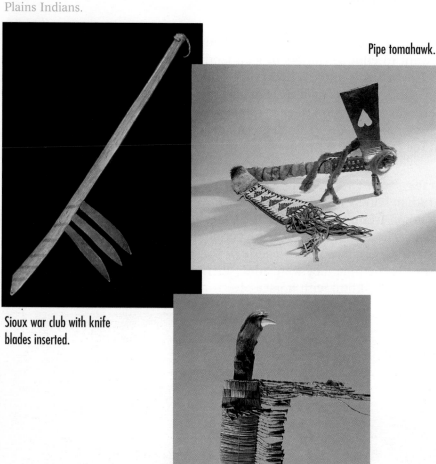

Pipe tomahawk.

Sioux war club with knife blades inserted.

Knife with metal blade; the handle was made from a bear's jaw. Knives like this were often used for scalping.

Weapons

White people brought to America the horses which transformed the lives of the Indians. They also brought guns, which turned those Indians which had them into even deadlier shots than they already were with bows and arrows. Indians, however, still used their traditional weapons.

The Indians' idea of bravery

The Plains Indians would not have understood the way in which the white man fought battles. The white man was expected to stand and fight until the last person was dead. The Indian gained honour when he touched an enemy, or when he brought an enemy's scalp back to camp. An Indian warrior did not want to die. What a waste that would be! Why risk being killed when he could slip away and live to fight another day?

In Source 5 a white man describes a Comanche's idea of bravery.

Source 5

Odie B. Faulk, *The Crimson Desert*, 1974.

The concept of bravery was completely different from that of the Europeans who came to live in the region. The Comanche thought it stupid to stand and fight when there was no chance of winning anything save honour; instead they would slink away from such a contest, to return another day to steal horses, booty and captives.

Counting coup

Touching the enemy with his hand or with a specially decorated stick was the highest honour which a warrior could win, especially if his enemy was alive. Each touch was called a coup. In doing this a warrior had risked his life. He had been amongst the enemy and had come back alive. The first man to touch an enemy in this way received the highest honour. There were lesser honours for those who touched the enemy second, third and fourth.

Source 6

E. A. Hoebel, *The Cheyenne*, 1978.

War has been transformed into a great game in which scoring against the enemy often takes precedence over killing him. The scoring is in the counting of coup – touching or striking an enemy with hand or weapons. Coups counted within an enemy encampment rank the highest of all. A man's rank as a warrior depends on two factors: his total 'score' in coups, and his ability to lead successful raids in which Cheyenne losses are low. Actual killing and scalping get their credit, too, but they do not rate as highly as the show-off deeds.

Source 7

Frederic Remington painted this picture of counting coup in the 1880s.

Scalping

There was another reason for the Indians' desire to avoid death in battle – fear of being scalped. This was one of the very worst things that could happen to an Indian. If your enemy had your scalp he also had your spirit. This would stop it going to the Happy Hunting Ground. When an Indian killed a person in battle, he scalped the person and carried the scalp back to camp. Scalps were dried and displayed in many ways – on top of tipi poles, hanging from horses' bridles, sewn into the seams of warrior's clothing. After a successful raid, Indians would have a Scalp Dance. The warriors and their women leaped, stamped and shouted around the scalps which had been brought back. Indians who had lost their scalps but had survived, could now restore their own spirits with the scalp of a dead enemy. Source 9 below explains why Comanche warriors were afraid of being scalped. Source 10 opposite describes Black Elk's first scalp.

Source 8

This engraving of an Indian scalping a dead cavalryman was made in 1892.

Source 9

Odie B. Faulk, *The Crimson Desert*, 1974.

The Comanche warrior out to count coup had no wish to die in battle, for he had to guard his immortal soul. He wanted horses, he desired plunder, and he would take women and children captive if he could, but he did not want to die. To die in battle was to risk scalping, and a scalped warrior could not enter heaven. Courage was the highest virtue amongst the Comanche, and they exhibited extraordinary courage when they carried off the bodies of their dead; but once a warrior's scalp had been taken, not even the bravest Comanche would touch the corpse.

Source 10

Black Elk in J. Neihardt, *Black Elk Speaks*, 1974

* **tremolo** A high-pitched vibrating noise made with the voice.

Men and horses were all mixed up and fighting in the water. Then we were out of the river, and people were stripping dead soldiers and putting the clothes on themselves. There was a soldier on the ground and he was still kicking. A Dakota rode up to me and said 'Boy, get off and scalp him.' I got off and started to do it. He had short hair and my knife was not very sharp. He ground his teeth, and then I shot him in the forehead and got his scalp.

I thought I would show my mother the scalp, so I rode over toward the hill where there was a crowd of women and children. When I got to the women on the hill they were all singing and making the tremolo* to cheer the men fighting across the river in the dust on the hill. My mother gave a big tremolo* just for me when she saw my first scalp.

Source 11

The feathers worn by Indian warriors all meant different things.

All Indian warriors wore feathers in their hair when they fought, and the successful ones could be spotted immediately by the way the feathers had been shaped.

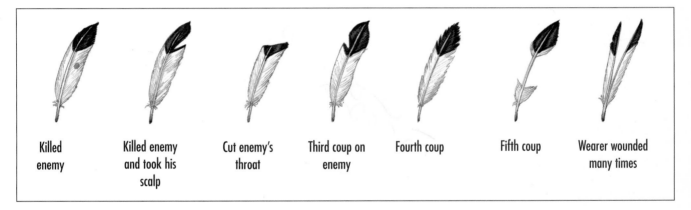

| Killed enemy | Killed enemy and took his scalp | Cut enemy's throat | Third coup on enemy | Fourth coup | Fifth coup | Wearer wounded many times |

Questions

1   Look at Source 2 and read Source 3.
   a Use your knowledge of the Plains Indians to explain when the Comanche would be most likely to use this trick.
   b George Catlin described this trick in a book published in 1844. What conclusions can you make from the fact that the Comanche were still teaching this trick to their boys 46 years later, when Frederic Remington produced his picture?

2   **a** Why was Black Elk's mother (Source 10) so pleased with what he had done?
   b Use the sources in this section and your own knowledge to explain:
      (i) why Indians believed it was important to scalp their enemies;
      (ii) why Indians believed it was important to avoid being scalped themselves.

3   **a** How was the Indians' idea of bravery different from that of white people?
   b Do you think this would lead to problems if they ever met in battle? Explain your answer.

Unit 2 Review

Questions

1   Many different tribes made up the 'Plains Indians'. Copy out the grid below. Work through Unit 2 and note down what you can find out about these particular tribes.

Name of tribe	What can you find out?
Apache	
Arapaho	
Cheyenne	
Comanche	
Iroquois	
Gros Ventre	
Mandan	
Sioux	

2   Were there more similarities than differences between the different nations of Plains Indians?

3   Many ideas and attitudes of the Plains Indians were very different from those of white people. Using the material in this unit and your own knowledge, fill in this grid:

	Indians	White people
Land Great Spirit Family Bravery		

Explain, using the headings in the first column of the grid, why there was likely to be conflict and misunderstanding between white people and Indians.

4   'The Plains Indians were cruel, blood-thirsty and uncivilised.' Explain, using the sources and information in this unit, whether or not you agree with this interpretation.

Unit 3 · Manifest destiny

In 1783 the USA was a very new country and only one of several nations on the continent of North America. (Look back to pages 5–6 to remind yourself why.) The leaders of the USA wanted to make the position of the young country, and the new Americans, secure. This American desire to control the whole of the continent of North America is called 'manifest destiny'. Americans gradually came to believe that they had a right to fill the continent with white Americans and to govern the whole of North America. They believed they had a right to fulfil their 'manifest destiny'.

Manifest destiny: the solution to a practical problem?

Filling the empty lands
In the introduction to this book you read how, by 1853, force, treaties and money had enabled the USA to own the whole of the continent of America from the Atlantic to the Pacific coast and from the Canadian to the Mexican borders. Americans were, however, afraid that Great Britain, France or Mexico would change their minds and try to take back the land which they had made over to the USA. One solution was to fill these

lands with men and women who were loyal to the young USA. These men and women would, it was argued, build homesteads and towns, railways and roads, and would farm, mine and trade. They would help to make the USA strong and prosperous, and safe from any enemies.

How was the USA to be governed?

In 1787 representatives from the new American states met in Philadelphia. These men, who were later called the 'Founding Fathers', had to try to work out how the thirteen states were to be governed. They had to decide on a system of government which would allow the states their independence yet, at the same time, enable them to work together as one country. It had to be possible, too, to extend this system of government into the lands beyond the Appalachian Mountains which were going to be settled by the new, white Americans. What they came up with was a federal republic. 'Federal' meant that all the various states were united into one country. 'Republic' meant that the Head of State was an elected president, not an hereditary monarch. This federal republic allowed for the individual states to make their own, local laws and so to keep some independence. The federal government made decisions for the whole country, such as whether or not to go to war and what taxes people should pay. Individual states made decisions such as whether or not to have the death penalty or whether slavery should continue. This system of government has continued to the present day.

Source 2

How the USA was governed in 1900.

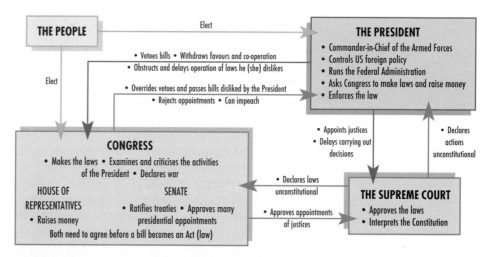

Manifest destiny and white supremacy

Long before independence in 1783 some Americans began to dream that the whole of the American continent would be settled by white Americans. Gradually Americans came to believe that this was the right and proper thing to happen. Not only was it right and natural, but it was something which clearly had to happen. It was, after all, their manifest destiny.

Thus when the wagons rolled westwards, and when the homesteaders began settling the Great Plains, Americans believed that the migrants were not just looking for new and fertile farmland. They were putting the American dream into action. They were beginning the final wave of migration which would end with the whole of America being lived in by white Americans. They believed that civilisation would be brought to the wilderness and to the 'savage' Indians who lived there. The manifest destiny of the American people was being fulfilled.

Source 3

These two maps show how the American West was settled between 1870 and 1890.

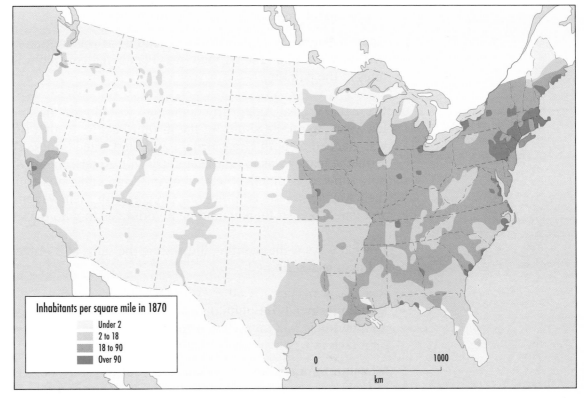

Inhabitants per square mile in 1870
- Under 2
- 2 to 18
- 18 to 90
- Over 90

0   1000
km

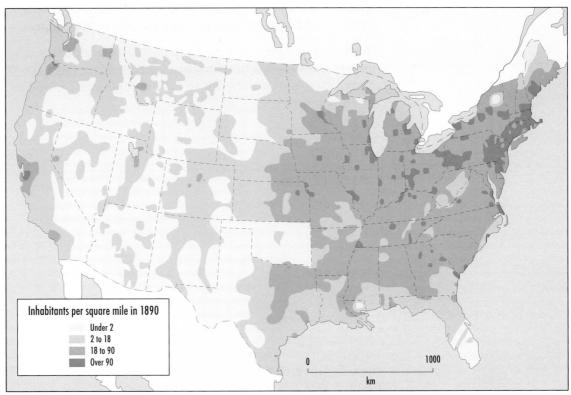

Inhabitants per square mile in 1890
- Under 2
- 2 to 18
- 18 to 90
- Over 90

0   1000
km

1   **a** What did some white Americans believe was the 'manifest destiny' of the American people?
    b How did they set about fulfilling this 'manifest destiny'?
    Use the information and all the sources in this chapter in your answer.

2   Look at Source 1 on page 33. Now read what was written by one of the first pioneers who crossed the Great Plains in a covered wagon like the ones in the painting:

P. H. Burnett, 'Recollections and Opinions of an Old Pioneer' in The Quarterly of the Oregon History Society, 1904.

> I saw that a great American community would grow up, in the space of a few years, upon the shores of the distant Pacific. At that time the country was claimed by both Great Britain and the United States. The only way to settle the matter was to fill the country with American citizens. If we could only show, by a practical test, that American emigrants could safely make their way across the continent to Oregon with their wagons, teams, cattle and families, then there would be no doubt as to who owned the country.

In what ways is the painting illustrating the same sort of feelings that the old man is describing?

3   Read these recipes:
Buffalo Jerky: Slice buffalo meat along the grain into strips one eighth of an inch thick, half an inch wide and two to three inches long. Hang them on a rack in a pan and bake at 200 degrees until dry.

Mormon Johnnycake: Combine two cups of yellow cornmeal, half a cup of flour, one teaspoon baking soda and one teaspoon salt. Stir in two cups of buttermilk and two tablespoons of molasses. Pour batter into a 9-inch pan and bake in a 400 degree oven for about 25 minutes.

These recipes were never actually used by the pioneers. They are modernised versions of what the pioneers might have cooked. Why would present-day Americans want to eat the same sort of food as that eaten by the early pioneers?

4   Copy this grid into your work-book:

Group	How they fulfilled the 'manifest destiny'
Mountain men	
Pioneers	
Mormons	
Miners	
Cattlemen	
Cowboys	
Homesteaders	

As you work through the units that follow, think about the ways in which the different groups of people might have fulfilled the idea of 'manifest destiny' and fill in the grid as you go along.

Unit 4 · Early settlers in the west

Mountain men

Why were mountain men important in the history of the West?

Source 1

'I took ye for an Injun' painted by Frederic Remington in 1890.

Source 1

'I took ye for an Injun' painted by Frederic Remington in 1890.

It is easy to see why Frederic Remington called his painting of two mountain men 'I took ye for an Injun'. The mountain man on the right does look very like one of the Indians you read about in Unit 2. Mountain men were expert hunters and trackers. Some of them married Indian women. Like Indians, mountain men knew about the ways of animals and the uses of plants. Sometimes they worked with Indians and sometimes they fought them.

Source 2

Two extracts from the journal of a mountain man, Osborne Russell, 1834–43.

We were completely surrounded. We cocked our rifles and started thro' their ranks into the woods which seemed completely filled with Blackfeet. An arrow struck White on the right hip joint. I hastily told him to pull it out and as I spoke another arrow struck me in the same place.

Source 2

> I cast my eyes down the mountain and discovered two Indians approaching. We grasped our guns. They quickly accosted us in the Snake tongue saying they were Shoshonies and friends to the whites. I invited them to approach and sit down. After our visitors had eaten and smoked, they pointed out the place where we could descend the mountain.

What was a mountain man's life like?

A mountain man's job was to trap and hunt animals for their fur. Most mountain men worked for trading companies, such as the Rocky Mountain Fur Company. Some worked for themselves, selling their furs and skins wherever they could get the best prices. They roamed the Sierra Nevada and the Rocky Mountains which bordered the Great Plains, setting their traps and getting to know every rock and waterfall, forest and swamp, pass and canyon. They saw the fertile plains and rich soils of Oregon and California beyond the Rocky Mountains.

Mountain men faced danger every day as they trapped and hunted wild animals. They also faced hunger and thirst, freezing cold and intense heat. They faced other dangers, too:

Source 3

From the diary of a mountain man, James Clyman.

* **lacerated** Torn with jagged edges.

> None of us having any surgical knowledge what was to be done one Said come take hold and he would say why not you … I asked the Capt. what was best he said one or two go for water and if you have needle and thread git it out and sew up my wounds round my head. [This I did] laying the lacerated* parts [of the ear] together as nice as I could with my hands. This gave us a lisson on the character of the grissily Bare which we did not forget.

Every year between 1815 and 1840, mountain men, trappers, traders and Indians held an enormous gathering called a 'Rendezvous' where they bought and sold furs. It was here that the mountain men talked of adventure and warned of dangers. They also talked of the rich, fertile lands which lay beyond the Rocky Mountains.

Source 4

An account written by an army surveyor who was sent to the West in the 1840s to map it scientifically.

* **delineate** Draw.

> Jim Bridger is one of the hardy race of mountain men who are now disappearing from the continent, being enclosed in a wave of civilisation. With a buffalo skin and a piece of charcoal he will map out any portion of this immense region, and delineate* mountains, streams, and the circular valleys called 'holes' with wonderful accuracy.

The news of good farming land west of the Rocky Mountains was told and re-told by traders travelling up and down the Missouri River. The news was spread eastwards among the farmers of Missouri, Mississippi, Ohio and Illinois. It was news that was to change the lives of thousands of people.

Many mountain men became guides to those who travelled west. They used their knowledge of the Great Plains, the Rocky Mountains and the Sierra Nevada to lead the early settlers safely into Oregon and California.

Questions		
	1	Read both the extracts from Osborne Russell's journal (Source 2). **a** Make a list of the differences between them. **b** Can you explain the differences between the extracts?
	2	Look again at Source 1. If the mountain men were so distrustful of the Indians, why did they want to look like them? Use the information in this section about mountain men in your answer.
	3	One of the ways in which Jim Bridger (Source 4) put his skills to good use was in guiding the wagon trains to Oregon and California. Was this the only real importance of the mountain men in the story of the settlement of the American West? Use the information and sources in this section to explain your answer.

Pioneers go to the far west

Why did the first pioneers go west?

Between 1839 and the end of the 1850s thousands of men, women and children deserted their homes in the eastern states. They left everything and nearly everyone they knew. They packed what they thought they needed into wagons and hand-carts, and began a difficult and dangerous journey across land which was unknown to them. Many did not survive. Many suffered terribly and kept the scars of the journey all their lives. What made them do it?

Many pioneers had heard of the mountain men's stories about rich, fertile land beyond the Sierra Nevada. They knew that the mountain men were willing to lead groups of migrants through the high passes to whatever lay beyond. The American government, too, wanted white Americans to settle the West before emigrants from other countries did so. But the men and women living in the eastern states didn't know this. They couldn't be certain that the land beyond the Rocky Mountains was rich and fertile. They did not know whether or not the mountain men were to be trusted. All the early migrants had were stories handed on by word of mouth. One thing, however, is certain. Men and women would not have risked all that they had and faced the dangers of the unknown, unless conditions at home in the eastern states were becoming so dreadful for them that nothing could be worse.

In 1837 a financial crisis hit eastern America. This left thousands of people bankrupt and many more without a job.

Source 1

This cartoon about the financial problems of 1837 is from *The Times*, New York.

At the same time, farmers in the eastern states who wanted their own land were being disappointed. There were simply too many of them trying to buy land. In Missouri, for example, the population grew from 14,000 in 1830 to 353,000 in 1840. Stories of rich, fertile empty lands in California and Oregon must have seemed very attractive. Their grandparents and great-grandparents had crossed the Appalachian Mountains to farm empty, fertile lands in Missouri and Arkansas. They, in their turn, would go west and cross the Great Plains and Rocky Mountains to the rich, lush lands beyond. So it was that the first pioneers left for Oregon in 1839 and for California in 1840. By 1850, which was the peak year for migration, some 55,000 people had travelled west.

How did the first pioneers get to the far west?

In the early days the first pioneers found their own way west. They were helped in the last stages of their journey by the mountain men who showed them the best and safest passes to use across the Rocky Mountains and the Sierra Nevada. Before long there were several tried and trusted trails which were safe enough, most of the time, for the pioneers to use without the help of guides. The most popular trails were the California Trail and the Oregon Trail. The fact, however, that these routes were well known did not mean that they were easy or even safe.

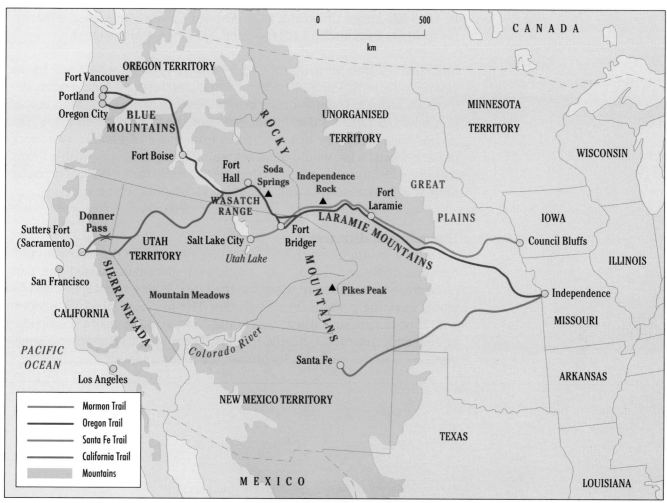

Source 2

Trails westward across the Great Plains.

Preparing for the journey west

Independence, a town on the border of Missouri, became very important to the first pioneers. Here they gathered before beginning the trek across the Great Plains and the long haul up and over the Rocky Mountains and the Sierra Nevada. It was at Independence that they checked through their supplies, and bought in fresh stocks of flour, sugar, blankets or candles – whatever they thought they needed for their journey and for beginning their new life the other side of the Great Plains and mountain ranges.

At Independence the pioneers waited until there were sufficient wagons to make up a reasonably-sized wagon train because it was dangerous to travel alone. The size of the wagon trains varied. It was sensible, for example, to have a number of strong, young men in the group as well as at least one person skilled in caring for sick people and two or three people who could hunt. Some people waited in Independence for many days until they had enough people with the right sorts of skills in their wagon train. They waited, too, until the prairie grass was rich and sweet enough to feed the animals. Then they would not have to take up valuable space by carting animal food with them. Most wagon trains ended up with at least twenty wagons and some had many more. One of the largest left Independence in 1843 with 1,000 men, women and children.

In 1845 Medorem Crawford, a 25-year-old Californian settler, wrote to his brothers back in the eastern states. This is part of his letter.

Source 3

Part of a letter from Medorem Crawford, 1845.

You must not start off with less than $75 dollars apiece, which will afford you with about $25 or $30 on hand when you arrive in Independence.

If you arrive at Independence before the party are ready to start, apply yourselves to some kind of business among the farmers to get cattle. Do not fail to secure a few head of heifers from one and a half to two years old or perhaps what would be better would be a young cow with a heifer calf some two months old. You should if possible each get a good young mule well broken to ride and a Spanish saddle, bridle and spurs.

Dangers and disasters

According to official estimates, 34,000 people died on the westward trails between 1840 and 1860. The plains and mountains tested the early pioneers in quite different ways. On the Great Plains, the wagons crawled along, covering perhaps 20 miles a day. The pioneers faced sandstorms and rain, hunger and thirst, quicksands and swollen rivers, stampeding buffalo and, sometimes, hostile Indians. There was, too, another enemy – disease – and the most deadly disease the pioneers faced was cholera.

Source 4

This was the type of wagon most used by the early pioneers.

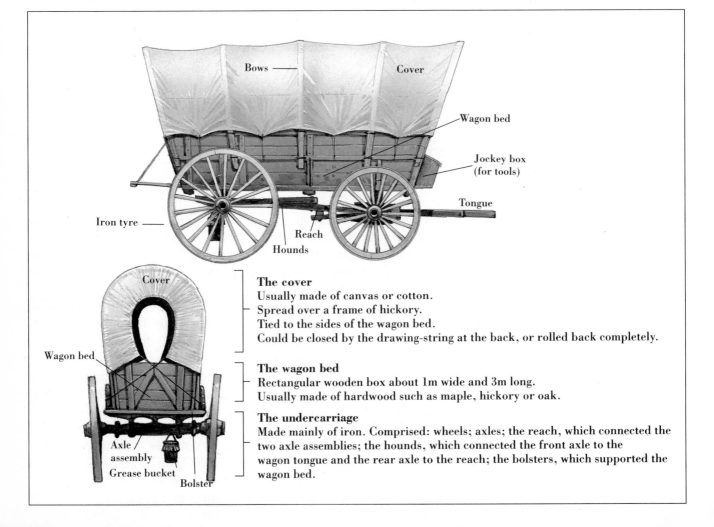

The cover
Usually made of canvas or cotton.
Spread over a frame of hickory.
Tied to the sides of the wagon bed.
Could be closed by the drawing-string at the back, or rolled back completely.

The wagon bed
Rectangular wooden box about 1m wide and 3m long.
Usually made of hardwood such as maple, hickory or oak.

The undercarriage
Made mainly of iron. Comprised: wheels; axles; the reach, which connected the two axle assemblies; the hounds, which connected the front axle to the wagon tongue and the rear axle to the reach; the bolsters, which supported the wagon bed.

Source 5

Extracts from Amelia Knight's diary. She and her husband left Iowa in 1853 for Oregon. They took with them their seven children: Plutarch, Seneca, Frances, Jefferson, Lucy, Almira and Chatfield.

* **out of humour** Bad-tempered.
* **ditto** The same.

Made our beds down in the wet and mud. Cold and cloudy this morning and everybody out of humour*. Seneca is half sick. Plutarch has broke his saddle girth. Husband is scolding. Almira says she wishes she was at home and I say ditto*....

We are creeping along slowly, one wagon after another, and the same thing over, out of one mud hole and into another all day. It has been raining all day long. The men and boys are all soaking wet and look sad and comfortless. The little ones and myself are shut up in the wagon from the rain. Take us all together and we are a poor looking set, and all this for Oregon....

Chatfield, the rascal, fell under the wagon. Somehow he kept from under the wheels. I never was so frightened in my life. I supposed Frances was taking care of him....

Chatfield quite sick with scarlet fever. A calf took sick and died before breakfast. Here we left, unknowingly, our Lucy behind. Not a soul had missed her until we had gone some miles when we stopped a while to rest the cattle; just then another train [of wagons] drove up behind us, with Lucy. It was a lesson to all of us....

Lost one of our oxen; he dropped dead in the yoke. I could hardly help shedding tears....

Passed a sleepless night as a good many of the Indians camped around us were drunk and noisy....

I was sick all night and not able to get out of the wagon in the morning. Yesterday my eighth child was born.

When they reached the Rocky Mountains the pioneers were weakened by their experiences on the Great Plains. But there was no time to rest. They had to push and pull wagons and possessions, children and animals through the high, narrow passes in the mountains. Here there was always the worry that the weather would close in on them and the autumn snows would leave them trapped in the Rocky Mountains or the Sierra Nevada. This did happen to a group of migrants led by George Donner.

The Donner party, 1846
The 40 adults and 41 children who made up the Donner party, led by George Donner, were very well-equipped. They had horses, oxen, cattle, wagons, money and luxuries like built-in beds and fancy foods. However, they made every mistake possible. Their first mistake was to leave Independence late in the year, after the other wagon trains had already left. Then they tried to catch up on lost time by leaving the trail and taking an untried short-cut. At the end of October 1846 they were trapped in deep snow on the wrong side of the Sierra Nevada. They decided to dig in for the winter. Conditions quickly became appalling. Animals died, food ran out, and men, women and children were left weak and close to starvation.

A small group of 15 adults, including two Indian guides, decided to try to battle through drifts and blizzards on foot to California to get help. The small amount of food they took with them quickly ran out. Four of the men were frozen to death in a snowstorm. Their companions roasted and ate them. The two Indian guides died a couple of days later. They were eaten as well. The remaining nine adults finally made it through to an Indian village. It had taken them 32 days.

Word quickly spread, and a rescue operation began to try to reach the trapped Donner party. Four separate groups set out from California. They risked their own lives struggling through blizzards and deep snows carrying packs of food for the men, women and children they hoped to find alive. They found what was left of the Donner party. They had survived by eating their dead friends and relations. Of the 81 people who had left Independence that summer, only 47 made it through to California. Not many people, however, suffered so badly:

Source 6

From a letter written by John Marsh, an early migrant, to several newspapers. It is dated 3 July 1840.

The difficulty of coming here is imaginary. The route I would recommend is from Independence to the hunter's rendezvous on Green River, thence to Soda Spring on Bear River, above the Big Salt Lake, thence to Portneuf, thence to Mary's River, down Mary's River until you come in sight of the gap in the great mountain, through that gap by a good road, and you arrive in the Plain of Joaquin, and down that river on a level plain through thousands of elk and horses, three or four days journey and you come to my house.

Journey's end

For most pioneers, however, their journey ended better than that of the Donner party.

Source 7

From a letter written by Nathaniel Ford to his family in the eastern states. Nathaniel reached Oregon in 1844.

We had a tedious and tiring trip: but I think we are well paid for our trouble; we are in the best country I have ever seen for farming and stock raising. The prairies are easily broken with two yoke of oxen, and harrows up fine for seeding. All the springs and streams are cool and fine flavoured.

Questions

1   Look carefully at Source 1 on page 40.
    a List all the troubles it shows.
    b How could the early pioneers be sure that they would not find these troubles waiting for them in Oregon and California?
    c How far does this source help to explain why people travelled west?

2   Read Sources 3, 6 and 7. How important would letters like this have been in persuading people to join friends and relations who had made the journey west to Oregon and California?

3   Amelia Knight and her family, the Donner party and John Marsh all travelled west to Oregon and California. How do you account for their very different experiences on the journey?

Source 8
This photograph is called 'Journey's End'. More than 30 horses are pulling a combine harvester through an Oregon wheatfield in the 1880s.

The Mormons: a special group of migrants?

The migrants from the east, struggling to cross plains and mountains, relied very much on the wisdom and advice of the mountain men. This was because the mountain men knew the land over which the migrants were travelling, and could help them avoid the many dangers. Not everyone, however, followed the advice of the mountain men.

Mormons and the mountain men
In 1847 the mountain man, Jim Bridger (see page 38), and two of his friends were travelling along a deserted trail which led, eventually, to the desolate wastes of the Great Salt Lake. They met up with a small group of men who were clearly the advance party of a much larger group.

Jim Bridger was horrified when he learned that their leader, Brigham Young, was planning to lead hundreds of men, women and children across the Great Plains to settle in the infertile wasteland around the Great Salt Lake. Desperately he tried to persuade Brigham Young to change his mind, and to choose instead the rich farmlands of Oregon. Brigham Young refused.

Finally, Jim Bridger made a promise: he would give Brigham Young $1,000 for the first bushel of grain grown in the valley of the Great Salt Lake. A thousand dollars was a lot of money. Jim Bridger must have been very sure he wouldn't have to pay!

Source 1

From part of a report written by William Clayton, one of the advance party of Mormons, to his leader, Brigham Young.

* **destitute** Totally without.

Mr Harris says he is well acquainted with the Bear River Valley and the region around the Salt Lake. From his description, which is very discouraging, we have little chance to hope for moderately good country anywhere in those regions. He speaks of the whole region being sandy, and destitute* of timber and vegetation except the wild sage.

Source 2

Sam Brennan, one of Brigham Young's group, sailed around Cape Horn to California and then crossed the Rocky Mountains to meet up with him. This is part of what Sam Brennan told him.

For Heaven's sake don't stop in this God forsaken land. Nobody on earth wants it. Come to California, to a land of sunshine and flowers.

The growth of the Mormons

Why did Brigham Young ignore the good advice of the mountain men and the reports from his own group? Why did he choose to make a living from poor, arid land? Why did he choose to settle so far away from other migrants?

Joseph Smith

Part of the answer to these questions lies in Palmyra, in New York State (see Source 3). Joseph Smith, the son of a poor farmer, claimed that in 1823 he dug some golden plates from a mountainside near his home in Palmyra. Four years later he began to translate the signs and symbols on these plates. He was helped by an angel called Moroni, who had earlier shown him where to dig on the mountainside. The golden plates were so secret that Joseph had to be very careful when translating them. He strung a blanket across the room in which he was working. He sat on one side of the blanket with the golden plates. On the other side of the blanket sat his wife and some friends. He called out the translation and his wife and friends wrote it down.

What they wrote down was a fantastic story of battles in America between the tribes of Israel. These battles began long before the birth of Christ and ended after his death. Mormon and his son Moroni were the only survivors of these battles. They wrote down, on golden plates, everything that had happened to them. They said that whoever found the plates would restore the church of Jesus Christ in America, and build up God's kingdom on earth ready for Christ's second coming.

Kirtland

The building of this 'kingdom' started in the city of Kirtland, Ohio. This was to be Zion, the 'heavenly city'. Mormons flocked there in their thousands. The Mormons bought land for farming and built homes in the city. They built a Mormon temple where they worshipped. They were encouraged to dedicate their land and property to the Mormon church, and to hand over their profits to the Mormon bishops. This money was used to help poor Mormons settle in Kirtland. Later, Mormons paid 10% of their income to their church. Soon there were more Mormons than non-Mormons living in Kirtland.

Mormons became involved in the financial and economic life of Kirtland. In 1837 Kirtland was hit by a massive financial crisis and the Mormon bank failed. Thousands of Mormons and non-Mormons lost money. The Mormons were angry with their leaders for failing to anticipate the crisis, but their anger was nothing compared with the fury on the non-Mormons who had lost money. Of course, many non-Mormon enterprises had failed as well, but the Mormons had told everyone they were God's chosen people. Non-Mormons had invested in Mormon enterprises because they thought they would never fail. It was not really surprising, therefore, that they blamed the Mormons when things went wrong. Joseph Smith and his Mormons were chased out of Kirtland. They were forced to flee to other Mormon settlements in the state of Missouri.

Source 3

Mormon journeys and settlements.

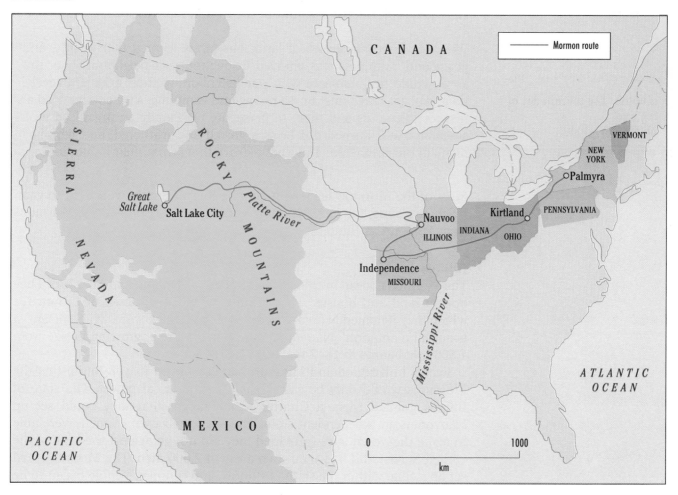

Missouri

At first the Mormons were successful in Missouri. They bought land, farmed and built. However, it was not long before the spread of Mormons into surrounding counties angered ordinary people. They were irritated by the Mormons' hard work and carefulness. They were suspicious of Mormon land purchases and did not believe Mormon claims that God wanted them to own the whole region. They suspected the Mormons of being friendly with the Indians and of wanting to abolish slavery.

Source 4

Missouri Intelligencer and *Boon's Lick Advertiser*, 10 August 1833.

But little more than two years ago, some two or three of these people made their appearance on the Upper Missouri and they now number some 1,200 souls in this country. Each autumn and spring pours forth its swarm amongst us, flooding us with the very dregs. The day is not far distant when the government of the county will be in their hands, when the sheriff, the Justices, and the county judges will be Mormons.

It was not surprising that violence broke out once again. This time, however, the Mormons organised themselves. They set up a secret police organisation called the Danites. The Danites were supposed to protect the Mormons from outside attack, and also to report to Mormon leaders any suspect activities of the Mormons themselves. Rumours of the existence of this secret organisation spread to non-Mormons and added to their fears. Here is Joseph Smith's account of the troubles in Missouri:

Source 5

W. Mulder and A. R. Mortensen *Amongst the Mormons*, 1958.

* **sabbath** The seventh day of the week.
* **habitation** Home.

We made large purchases of land, our farms teemed with plenty, and peace and happiness was enjoyed throughout our neighbourhood. But as we could not associate with our neighbors in their midnight revels, their sabbath* breaking, horse racing and gambling, they commenced at first to ridicule us and them to persecute us. Finally an organised mob assembled and burned our houses, tarred and feathered, and whipped many of our bretheren, and finally drove them from their habitations*.

Most of the Mormon leaders, including Joseph Smith, were sent to gaol. Brigham Young, the only Mormon leader not in prison, led the Mormons from Missouri to Illinois.

Illinois

The Mormons began in Illinois as they had in Kirtland and Missouri. They bought land and houses. They rebuilt the decaying town of Commerce which they renamed Nauvoo. 'Nauvoo' is a Hebrew word which means 'a beautiful plantation'. Nauvoo certainly did flourish, growing in size from 1,500 inhabitants in 1842 to 11,057 in 1845.

Events in Kirtland and Missouri had convinced Joseph Smith that the Mormons would only be safe if they held political power. The state of Illinois granted them a Charter which meant that they could set up Nauvoo as an independent state. They had their own council, were able to make their own laws (provided they did not go against the laws of the United States) and had their own army of 2,000 men. The Mormons had set up a state within the state of Illinois, and ordinary people began to be afraid. They were afraid of the power of the Mormons and of the Mormon army. They grew even more afraid when they found out that Mormon men could have more than one wife at a time. This was called polygamy. Ordinary people were afraid there would be a population explosion of Mormons and they would be outnumbered. Many Mormons, too, believed that having more than one wife at a time was wrong. They said openly that the Book of Mormon did not allow it. They became upset and angry when they discovered that Joseph Smith had more than one wife.

The situation was already explosive. Then Joseph Smith announced his intention to stand for election as President of the USA and people in Illinois prepared for war against the Mormons. Joseph Smith was thrown into prison and in June 1844 died at the hands of the mob. The state governor withdrew Nauvoo's Charter and told all Mormons to leave the state.

The decision to move west

Brigham Young, the new leader of the Mormons, decided that the Mormon's Zion would be built in the desolate and deserted foothills of the Rocky Mountains, on land surrounding the Great Salt Lake. This was land that no one else could possibly want. Here the Mormons would be free from persecution and could live out their lives and their beliefs in the ways they thought best.

Source 6

An American cartoon from the 1840s, making fun of polygamy.

The Mormons had to leave Nauvoo in a hurry. This meant they were not able to spend as much time as other migrants in thinking, planning and preparing for the long and difficult journey which lay ahead of them. They spent the winter of 1845 making what preparations they could. However, when mobs began looting their houses in the spring of 1846, the Mormons had no choice but to leave as quickly as they could. They were forced to sell up at knock-down prices and move on yet again. The last Mormon wagon train left Nauvoo in September 1846.

The Mormons, though, had three enormous advantages which other migrants did not have. They had earlier experiences of moving all that they had and of starting again somewhere else. They had learned to live and work together as a group. They also had Brigham Young as their leader.

Brigham Young

Brigham Young's first task was to organise the move of 15,000 men, women and children 2,250 km into unknown, dangerous territory. He had to help them survive a journey for which they were poorly prepared. To do this successfully they had to be well organised. Brigham Young was an excellent organiser. He divided the Mormons into manageable groups, each with a leader. He insisted upon strict discipline and routine throughout the journey. Everyone had a part to play, and knew what was expected of them. Brigham Young taught them how to drive their wagons in parallel lines, and how to form up into circles at night for safety. He set up resting places along the route. This broke the journey up into manageable sections, and made sure that neither animals nor people became too exhausted. Source 7 shows one Mormon family resting during its journey to Utah.

Source 7

The Byington family were photographed in 1867 as they travelled into the state of Utah. They were Mormons. They are, left to right at the back: Sarah (age 11) Elizabeth (age 6) Nancy (age 37) Nancy (age 17) and Hannah (age 30). Left to right in the front: Hyrum (age 8) Janette (age 2) and Joseph Henry (age 39). The elder Nancy and Hannah were Joseph Henry's wives.

Brigham Young's advance party followed the ruts made by the wheels of the ill-fated Donner party's wagons. Would their journey end as unhappily? They reached the top of a pass. There, in front of them, stretching as far as they could see, were the deep blue waters of the sterile Great Salt Lake. Brigham Young is supposed to have said 'It is enough. This is the right place. Drive on.' His sister-in-law, Harriet, arriving a few days later, felt differently:

Source 8

Written by Harriet, Brigham Young's sister-in-law, in her diary

* **desolate** Deserted and lifeless.
* **forsaken** Uninhabited.

My feelings were such as I could not describe. Everything looked gloomy and I felt heart sick. Weak and weary as I am, I would rather go a thousand miles farther than remain in such a desolate* and forsaken* spot as this.

The advance party reached the Great Salt Lake in July 1847. The main party arrived there in August, but Mormons arrived almost continually after that (apart from during the winter months) as wagon train after wagon train got through to the valley of the Great Salt Lake.

Settling in to the Salt Lake Valley

To arrive in the Salt Lake Valley was not the end of the story. In many ways the Mormons' problems were just beginning. Brigham Young was going to need all his powers of leadership and organisation if Mormons were to survive and flourish.

First, the land on which they had settled had to be shared fairly between Mormon families. Here Brigham Young explains how this will be done:

Source 9

Brigham Young, 1847.

* **cultivate** To use for growing crops.

No man can ever buy land here, for no one has any land to sell. But every man shall have his land measured out to him, which he must cultivate* in order to keep it. There shall be no private ownership of the streams that come out of the canyons, nor the timber that grows on the hills. These belong to the people: all the people.

The Mormons had to grow crops if they were to survive. The soil, although it looked rich, was very, very dry. Water was desperately needed and the Lake was far too salty to be used. The Mormons set up a committee to plan and dig irrigation ditches, and to see that no one took more water than they needed. Brigham Young's decision that the land belonged to everyone meant that the Church leaders could control how much each family was allowed to farm. It also meant that they could control the building of Salt Lake City, and decide how much land was to be given to shops and houses, to the Temple and Meeting Place, and to other public buildings.

Self-sufficiency

Brigham Young knew very well how hostile many ordinary people were to the Mormons. He did not want them to have to depend upon a hostile outside world for the goods they needed. He therefore decided that the Mormons should become self-sufficient. This meant that they would produce for themselves everything they needed. This included not only food and clothing but also manufactured goods. Clearly, Mormons with lots of different skills were needed to come and live in the Salt Lake Valley. Brigham Young therefore set up a Perpetual Emigration Fund to provide money for poor Mormons from elsewhere in America and from Europe to make the journey. Thousands did, and gradually the Mormons became self-sufficient, as Sources 10 and 11 show.

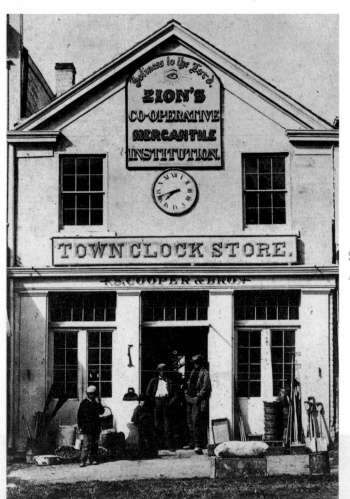

Source 10
A Mormon store in Salt Lake City, 1857.

Source 11
A contemporary engraving of Salt Lake City in 1873.

The politically independent Mormon state

Brigham Young wanted to make certain that the Mormons were free to follow their own customs and beliefs without outside interference. This meant that they had to be politically independent. When the Mormons settled in Salt Lake Valley in 1847 it was part of Mexico, not the USA. When the war between Mexico and the USA ended in 1848, large amounts of Mexican territory, including the valley of the Great Salt Lake, became US territory. Brigham Young promptly applied to the US government for the Mormon lands to become an independent state within the USA. This new state was to be called 'Deseret', which means 'Land of the Honey-bee'. The Mormons chose this name because they thought of themselves as being as busy as bees.

In Washington, however, the US government had other ideas. All the old fears about the Mormons returned, and the government refused to allow them to have their own state. Instead it decided to give the land the status of a territory. This meant that the Mormons could not have their own representatives in Washington. Instead they would have government officials running their affairs. Furthermore, the territory was not as large as the Mormons had hoped, and did not contain a port. The government also rejected the name 'Deseret'. It decided that the new territory was to be called 'Utah' after the Ute Indians who lived there.

The territory of Utah

The US government appointed Brigham Young to be the first Governor of the Territory of Utah. However, Mormons were not allowed to make their own laws. The law was administered by judges from Washington and the territory was run by government officials. Brigham Young did not always agree with what Washington wanted to do in Utah. It was hardly surprising that there was a great deal of tension between Brigham Young and the US government. To make matters worse, many Mormons chose to ignore the government and kept to their own laws and practices. Reports reached Washington of government officials being insulted, beaten and even killed; of judgements made in law courts being ignored; and of Brigham Young using the Danites to crush all opposition from non-Mormons.

Something had to be done. Clearly Brigham Young could not allow Mormon beliefs and practices to be destroyed. Equally clearly, the US government could not allow its rule to be ignored. In 1857 the US government sent a non-Mormon governor to Salt Lake City to replace Brigham Young. With the new governor it sent 1,500 soldiers.

The tension mounted to fever pitch. Bloodshed seemed inevitable. But when blood was shed, it was shed in an unexpected quarter. In September 1857 a wagon train of 140 migrants was massacred at Mountain Meadows, some 500 km to the south-west of Salt Lake City. The Mormons blamed the Indians. The non-Mormons blamed the Danites. No one knows for certain who was to blame. However, the massacre made the US government change its mind. It decided to try to get a peaceful settlement with the Mormons.

The US government agreed to let the Mormons live their own lives in their own way. It was not, however, prepared to let the Territory of Utah become a state until the Mormon church agreed to ban polygamy. (This happened in 1890.) In return, the Mormons agreed to accept a non-Mormon governor.

Questions

1 **a** Why did the Mormons leave Kirtland?
  b Look at Source 5. Did the Mormons leave Missouri for the same reasons that they left Kirtland?
  c What does Source 5 show about Joseph Smith's attitude to non-Mormons?

2 Look at Sources 4 and 6. Explain why ordinary people hated and feared the Mormons.

3 Many people opposed the Mormons. When this happened, Joseph Smith moved them to towns which he hoped would be more friendly. Brigham Young, on the other hand, moved the Mormons to land which no one could possibly want. Which of these two decisions was the wiser? Why?

4 **a** How did the US government try to control the Mormons?
  b Why, in the end, did the US government decide to let the Mormons live their own lives in their own way?

Were the gold miners really migrants?

The early pioneers, including the Mormons, made the long journey westwards because they believed they could make a better life for themselves and their families. There was, however, another group of people travelling west to California. They were not travelling with their families. Few of them crossed the Great Plains and Rocky Mountains in organised groups. Their main reason for going to California was not to settle down.

Gold rush!
Early in 1848 gold was discovered in California. Quickly the news reached the eastern states and the rest of the world. Within a few months 40,000 men were reported to be crossing the Great Plains, and 60 ships carrying eager would-be miners left ports in America and Europe bound for California. The gold rush had begun! Many of the men were not proper miners at all. They had all kinds of jobs in offices, factories and farms, and many had no jobs at all. But they all wanted to get rich quickly. Some of them did not survive the journey. Most of them did not find gold and wandered back home or drifted from job to job and mine to mine. Some men, however, did strike gold and became extremely rich indeed. It

was stories of these lucky strikes which kept men hoping that tomorrow, maybe, they would be the ones to strike it lucky.

Gradually, though, the gold in California (which was near the surface and therefore easy to mine) was exhausted. Then, in 1858–59, gold was discovered in the Pikes Peak region of the Rocky Mountains. Miners, and men hoping to be miners, began the great journey eastwards to the Rocky Mountains. Gold and silver was found in Idaho (1860) Montana (1862), Arizona (1863) and in the Black Hills of Dakota (1874). This last strike was to have a dramatic and terrible effect upon the Indians living there (see pages 109–110). It is important for now to realise that the miners, having first followed the traditional pattern of travelling from east to west, now reversed the pattern and travelled from west to east.

Miners and mining towns

Luck played an important part in the early days of the gold rush. Most of the first miners were not really miners at all. They did not know how to mine properly, and so they concentrated on looking for loose gold near

Source 1

A contemporary painting of men panning for gold during the Californian gold rush of 1849.

the surface. They lived in mining camps which sprang up quickly when gold was thought to be in a certain area, and which died out just as quickly when the miners moved on. In the 1850s the surface gold in California was almost exhausted, and the professional miners moved in. These men had had experience and training in mining. Many of them had worked in the tin and gold mines of Cornwall in England, and were able to sink and work deep mines. They were backed by eastern businessmen who put money into machinery and mills, and who made gold mining a profitable industry. These professional miners built and lived in permanent mining towns, and brought their wives and families with them.

The mining towns in the Rocky Mountains and on the edges of the Great Plains grew up quickly. They grew before the federal or state law (see page 34) could reach them and so brought with them problems of law and order. They also speeded up the settlement of the West. The gold needed to be moved quickly from the mines. The mining families needed food and manufactured goods. Not only did this mean that roads and railways had to be built, but it also meant that more and more people were attracted to the idea of moving and settling in the West.

HO FOR THE YELLOW STONE
AND — THE
GOLD MINES OF IDAHO!

A NEW AND VERY LIGHT DRAUGHT STEAMER WILL LEAVE
SAINT LOUIS FOR BIGHORN CITY!
THE JUNCTION OF BIGHORN AND YELLOW STONE RIVERS,
SATURDAY, APRIL 2D, AT 12 O'CLOCK M.

Parties taking this route save 400 miles river transportation and over 100 miles land transportation. Bighorn City being by a good wagon road from Virginia City 200 and from Bannack City 205 miles.

I WILL ALSO SEND TWO LIGHT DRAUGHT SIDE-WHEEL STEAMERS
TO FORT BENTON

One leaving at the same time, and the second about fifteen days later. I am prepared to contract for Freight and Passage either to Bighorn City or Fort Benton.
refer to W. B. DANCE, JAS. STEWART and N. WALL, Virginia City, or to M. MANDEVILLE, Bannack City.

For Freight or Passage apply to **JOHN G. COPELIN,**
Care JOHN J. ROE & CO., St. Louis, Mo

Questions

1 a What can be learned from Source 1 about gold mining in California?
   b Use this source and the information in this section to explain why so few men made fortunes from gold mining.

2 How did gold mining speed up the settlement of the West?

1   Why did people go west?

Group	When did they go?	Where did they go?	Why did they go?
Pioneers Mormons Miners			

Copy the grid above. Using the information in Unit 4 fill in the blank columns to answer the questions.

2   Look back to Source 8 on page 45.
Does this photograph prove that the pioneers were right to move west?

3   a Using the information in this unit, explain the importance of the following to the people who travelled to the West:
(i) advice from the mountain men
(ii) a well-built wagon
(iii) people with expertise in the wagon train
(iv) a desire to leave the old way of life behind and begin a new life.
b What other factors were important in making sure people reached the far west safely?
c What, in your judgement, was the most serious problem facing people travelling across the Great Plains, Rocky Mountains and Sierra Nevada to the far west?

4   Read the section under the heading 'The Mormons: a special group of migrants?' (pages 45–46) again.
a What sort of leadership did Joseph Smith give theMormons?
b What sort of leadership did Brigham Young give the Mormons?
c Who was the more successful leader: Joseph Smith or Brigham Young?
Now read about the Donner party on pages 43–4.
d What kind of a leader was George Donner?
Remember always to give hard evidence to back up what you write.

5   Remember to look back to question 4 on page 36 and begin filling in the grid.

Unit 5 · The cattle kingdom: cattlemen and cowboys

Many Americans believed that no one would ever settle on the Great Plains. Colonel Richard Dodge, who knew the Great Plains well when he was an adult, was taught when he was a child that they were unexplored.

Source 1

Colonel R. I. Dodge, *Hunting Grounds of the Great West*, 1877.

When I was a schoolboy my map of the United States showed between the Missouri River and the Rocky Mountains a long and broad white blotch, upon which was printed in small capitals THE GREAT AMERICAN DESERT – UNEXPLORED.

At the start of the great push westwards, the Great Plains were an obstacle which had to be crossed. Then, gradually, white men began to see ways of using the Great Plains. At first they drove cattle over the Great Plains to markets where they were sold. Then they began rearing cattle on the Great Plains themselves. The one thing that made all this possible was the building of a railroad that connected the east and west coasts of the USA.

Source 2

This map shows the spread of cattle ranching and the first trans-continental railroad in North America.

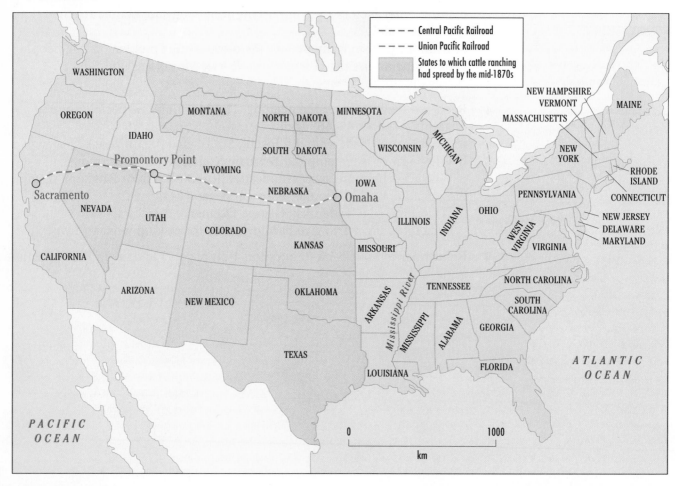

Legend:
- – · – · Central Pacific Railroad
- – – – Union Pacific Railroad
- States to which cattle ranching had spread by the mid-1870s

WASHINGTON, OREGON, IDAHO, MONTANA, NORTH DAKOTA, SOUTH DAKOTA, MINNESOTA, WISCONSIN, MICHIGAN, NEW HAMPSHIRE, VERMONT, MAINE, MASSACHUSETTS, NEW YORK, RHODE ISLAND, CONNECTICUT, Promontory Point, WYOMING, IOWA, Omaha, PENNSYLVANIA, Sacramento, NEVADA, UTAH, NEBRASKA, ILLINOIS, INDIANA, OHIO, NEW JERSEY, DELAWARE, MARYLAND, COLORADO, WEST VIRGINIA, VIRGINIA, CALIFORNIA, KANSAS, MISSOURI, ARIZONA, OKLAHOMA, NEW MEXICO, ARKANSAS, TENNESSEE, NORTH CAROLINA, SOUTH CAROLINA, Mississippi River, MISSISSIPPI, ALABAMA, GEORGIA, TEXAS, LOUISIANA, FLORIDA

ATLANTIC OCEAN

PACIFIC OCEAN

0 — 1000 km

Building the east-west railroad

Part of a poster advertising the opening of the first trans-continental railroad, 10 May 1869.

Before the 1860s all railroads stopped at the Mississippi and Missouri rivers. By 1890 railroads spanned the whole of North America. How had this happened? The first railroad beyond the Mississippi-Missouri rivers was not built to help travellers, but to help industry. The idea was that it should connect the industrial states of the east with the valuable land and resources of the West. Building began in 1866. The Union Pacific Railroad Company began laying track at Omaha in Iowa and the Central Pacific Railroad Company began at Sacramento in California. They met at Promontory Point, Utah, in May 1869. The problems involved in building these lines were enormous.

What were the problems?

Money
The first problem was money. The railroad companies needed money to buy land, pay the workers and buy locomotives and wagons. They had to persuade their shareholders* (see below) to invest in an enterprise that might at first seem risky and which might not earn money for the first few years.

Difficult land
The other problems were caused by the land which the railroad had to cross: mountains, valleys and deserts. All these stretched the skills of the engineers and construction workers to the limit. The labourers lived and worked in squalid conditions. They faced hostile Indians, driving rain and snow. They depended on food brought hundreds of kilometres to them. They died in their hundreds. Even so, they built fast and they built well. They built about 11 km of track each day on the Great Plains, and built the Dale Creek Bridge, which was 38 m high and 150 m long, in one month. At that time and under those conditions, it was an amazing achievement.

* **shareholder** A person who buys shares in a company and who is paid money, called a dividend, from that company's profits. If, in any one year, the company doesn't make a profit, then the shareholders don't get paid a dividend for that year.

Rival railroad companies

The meeting of the Union Pacific railroad and the Central Pacific railroad almost didn't happen. The two railroad companies were great rivals, and, as the lines neared each other, they built the tracks faster and faster. The moment of meeting came – and went. The two crews passed each other, frantically laying track. At that point the government stepped in and ordered the lines to meet at Promontory Point. A great ceremony was held when the lines were finally joined up. The last nail to be driven into a sleeper was made of gold. Two locomotives were driven together, nose to nose. The gold nail, of course, was removed immediately, but that didn't alter the fact that now America had its first trans-continental railroad.

Source 4

Railroads meet! The 'Golden Spike' ceremony at Promontory Point, Utah, on 10 May 1869.

Indians

The Indians remained a problem for the white men, just as the white men did for the Indians. Indians had harassed the white men as they were building the railroad. The first white pioneers who had crossed the Great Plains had not stayed. They hadn't altered the way the Great Plains looked and what happened on them. This was different. The Indians were worried that their hunting grounds might be taken away from them. They were very frightened of the huge, noisy 'iron horse' that crossed the Great Plains, billowing smoke and pulling carriages full of people.

Travelling by railroad

Other railroads were soon built on the Great Plains with the help of government grants of land and money. By 1893 there were six companies that connected the Mississippi-Missouri rivers with the Pacific coast. However, travelling by train was not always easier than travelling by wagon, as this source shows.

Source 5

Major General Grenville M. Dodge, *How we built the Union Pacific Railway*, 1911.

* **sheds** (Here) wooden covers built over the railroad to stop snow from piling up on the track.

We had no means of fighting the snows in the Laramie Plains except by fences and sheds* and none were put up until the year 1870, so that when the heavy snows fell in the winter of 1869–70, it caught six of our trains west of Laramie that were snowed in there for some weeks.... These six trains...were supplied with sledges and snow shoes from Laramie. They had with them, in charge of the six trains, Mr H M Hoxie, the Assistant Superintendent, who managed to get the trains together, but the blizzards were so many and so fierce that it was impossible for men to work out in the open.... Mr Hoxie handled his forces with great ability and fed and entertained his passengers. In one train was an opera company bound for California, that Mr Hoxie used to entertain the passengers with, so that when the trains reached Salt Lake City, the passengers held a meeting and passed resolutions complimentary to Mr Hoxie and the Union Pacific in bringing them safely through.

The old days of the pioneers, when wagon trains struggled slowly through blizzards or blazing heat to cross the Great Plains and the Rocky Mountains sometimes must not have seemed so far away.

Questions

1   The railroad company faced many problems in building the railroad. Which were the most serious and why?

2   Look at Source 3. The railroad company seems very proud to announce the opening of the railroad. Why do you think this was?

3   Read Source 5 again and then look back at the story of the Donner party (Unit 4, pages 43–4). What was the same and what was different about the two journeys?

4   Why was it important to white Americans to have a railroad that joined the eastern states to the west coast? Use the information and sources in this section and in Unit 3 in your answer.

Texans on the trail

Some of the Spanish who conquered North and Central America in the sixteenth century settled on land bordering the Gulf of Mexico around the River Nueces. They brought with them cattle and horses. The horses (see page 8) changed forever the way of life of the Plains Indians. The cattle were to create wealth for the cattlemen who owned them and a whole new way of life for the men who looked after them: the cowboys.

Who were the ranchers?

The first ranchers

The Indians who lived in what is now Texas were friendly, so the Spanish who settled there called it *tejas*, which is from the Spanish word for 'friend'. From this came the modern name 'Texas'. Here the Spanish settlers began cattle ranching. Their cattle were big, fierce, hardy animals with a thick, tough hide that was usually black or brown in colour. The steers (males) had horns with an enormous spread of up to 1.5 m. Herds of cattle wandered freely over the rich, plentiful grass. The climate was mild and there was plenty of water. These conditions were ideal for breeding, and the herds soon became very large indeed. These wandering herds of Longhorn cattle had to be rounded up from time to time, and so the Spanish ranchers employed Indians and half-breeds (people who were half-Indian and half-white) to do this. These vaqueros (from the Spanish word *vaca*, meaning 'cow') were skilled riders. They were expert at roping cattle with *la reata* (lariat), a rawhide rope with a noose that could be pulled tight.

The first cattle trails

After the war between the United States and Mexico (see page 5) the white American Texans took over the herds of Longhorn cattle. They decided that if they were to make any money at all they would have to drive the cattle north, out of Texas. In Texas there was plenty of meat, but in the north there were many people who wanted to buy large stocks of meat. The first cattle 'trails' began in 1837 when cowboys drove herds of between 300 and 1,000 cattle to markets in cities of the south-east. In 1842, cowboys blazed a trail to New Orleans; in 1850 to California and in 1856 to Chicago. These cattle drives were, however, not regular and were fairly disorganised affairs. But they were the start of something bigger and far more profitable.

Ranchers on the trails north

The Civil War between the northern states and the southern Confederate states began in 1861. This put an end to the early trails, because many Texans went off to fight for the Confederate armies. When the war ended in 1865 and the Texans returned, they found the herds of cattle running wild. With few people to look after them, the Longhorns had toughened up in order to survive, and had bred until there were about 5 million of them roaming the grasslands of Texas. However, the returning cattlemen knew that the growing cities of the industrial north would buy as much beef as they could get. They knew, too, that they could get about $40 per head of cattle in the north, ten times the price beef fetched in Texas. They rounded up the cattle, hired cowboys and began to organise regular drives to the northern cities.

Source 2

Map to show cattle trails and cow-towns.

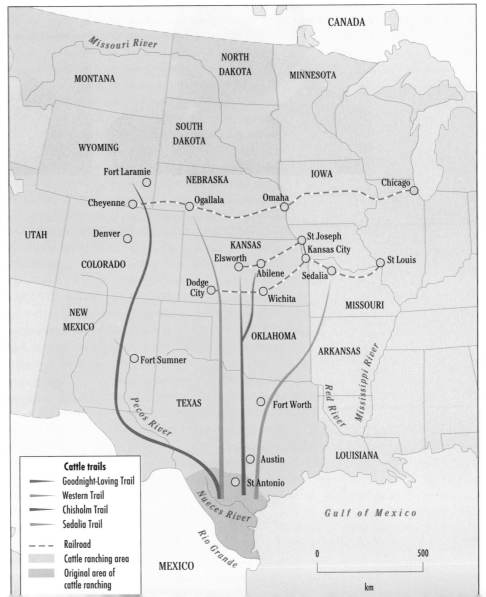

The cattlemen soon realised that if they drove their cattle 800 km or so north to the new railroad, they could get them quickly to the growing towns in the mid-west and to those in the east. In 1866, about 260,000 head of cattle from Texas crossed the Red River, making for Sedalia. Sedalia was a rail-head on the Missouri-Pacific railroad. There the cattle were loaded into wagons and taken east to St Louis and then north to Chicago.

Charles Goodnight and Oliver Loving: a success story

Source 3 Charles Goodnight.

Source 4 Oliver Loving.

When Charles Goodnight returned home to Texas after the Civil War, he found that his cattle were running wild. He also found that his herd had increased in size enormously. By the spring of 1866, Goodnight had 8,000 head of cattle. However, instead of driving part of the herd to the nearest rail-head to reach cattle markets in the east, he did something entirely different. He had heard that government troops were holding around 7,000 Navaho Indians captive near Fort Sumner in New Mexico. He had also heard that the Indians were close to starvation. Here was an opportunity not to be missed! Charles Goodnight teamed up with Oliver Loving, an experienced cattle driver. They were going to try to reach Fort Sumner, where they would sell meat to feed the starving Indians.

Goodnight and Loving hired 18 cowboys and selected 2,000 cattle from Goodnight's herd. Goodnight also designed what is said to be the first chuck wagon to carry all the equipment and supplies they would need on this new drive. They knew there would be problems with this route. Not only might they be attacked by Indians, but they would be without water for a lot of the drive. The lack of water nearly ruined their expedition. Cows, steers and men all suffered. Many animals died before they reached the Pecos River, rest and lush grass. However, when they reached Fort Sumner they still had 1,700 head of cattle to sell to the government. The starving Indians were fed and Goodnight and Loving made a huge profit.

Problems with the cattle trails

It was not all easy, though. In south-east Kansas, south Missouri and north Arkansas the cattle and their cowboys were met by armed mobs. People were afraid of the deadly Texas fever that came from a tick carried by the Longhorns. The Longhorns themselves were immune to it, but the disease they carried could cause havoc in other cattle. Others in the mob were cattle rustlers and robbers who were prepared to fight and kill to get the Longhorns for themselves. Many cattlemen then started using routes further west, reaching the railroad at St Joseph, Missouri, for the rail journey to Chicago. In the end, these routes proved safer and were used on most future drives.

There were problems with all the established cattle trails. The Goodnight-Loving trail was the furthest west and so avoided the hostile mobs in Kansas and Missouri, and, to a certain extent, hostile Indians. However, it did have problems with water supplies and was not much use to those cattlemen wanting to sell beef in the eastern states. These cattleman had to use the eastern trails to the various rail-heads. They faced hostile whites and hostile Indians and, once they got east of Sedalia (see Source 2) the grass provided very poor grazing.

Joseph McCoy and Abilene: the solution to a problem

Joseph McCoy, a cattle dealer from Illinois, found the ideal solution:

Source 5

W P Webb, *The Great Plains*, 1931.

* **drover** Cattleman.

> The plan was to establish a market whereat the Southern drover* and the Northern buyer would meet upon equal footing, and both be undisturbed by mobs or swindling thieves.

McCoy decided he would build a town specially for cattle dealing. The place he chose was Abilene, on the Kansas-Pacific railroad. Abilene was then nothing more than a dozen log huts, but it had all the grass and water needed when thousands of cattle gathered there, waiting to be sold. It was also, as McCoy himself said, 'the farthest point east at which a good depot for the cattle business could be made.'

McCoy worked furiously to make Abilene into the first cow-town. He had timber sent in and built offices, cattle pens and a small hotel. In 1867 cattlemen took about 36,000 cattle along the Chisholm Trail from St. Antonio to Abilene. By 1870 the number of cattle had grown to over 300,000 and Abilene had three more hotels and ten saloons. Between 1867 and 1881, nearly 1.5 million head of cattle passed through Abilene. McCoy had been right about the need for a cattle town. More were to follow the success of Abilene. Source 6 on page 66 shows just how busy these towns became.

Source 6
Loading cattle into Kansas stock cars in Wichita, 1874.

Questions

1   Why did cattlemen and cowboys use and develop the cattle trails?

2   What was a cow-town? Why didn't the cowboys simply keep on driving their cattle to the rail-heads?

Ranching on the Great Plains

New cow-towns were built as the railroad went further west – Dodge City, Wichita and Elsworth. New trails were blazed to connect with the railroad at these points. They were enormously successful. For example, between 1875 and 1885 about a quarter of a million head of cattle passed through Dodge City to be taken by railroad to places like Chicago and Kansas City where they were slaughtered. However, the last great drives north were in 1886. By 1895 the drives had ended.

Why did the cattle drives end?

The railroads across the Great Plains made many cattlemen rich. They had also brought people who began to settle and to farm the Great Plains (see Unit 6). The settlers' farms began to block the trails.

Source 1

J. G. McCoy, *Historic Sketches of the Cattle Trade of the West and South-west*, 1874.

His first care will be to select a location that has running water, as much timber and other shelter as possible, with a large tract of unsettled and untillable country surrounding it.

The Indians, too, made life difficult for the cattlemen. In 1868 the US government had granted land to the Indians (see Unit 8 pages 105–6) Now the Indians began to make the cowboys pay to drive the cattle across Indian land.

The cattlemen began to think that it would be easier to raise cattle on the Great Plains. In 1870 Charles Goodnight bought a plot of land on the Arkansas River near Pueblo in Colorado, and used cattle driven up from Texas to stock his range there. Others followed his example. By 1880 cattle ranches had been set up in six territories in the northern Plains, all stocked with Texas Longhorns.

Source 2

Figures for the cattle industry on the northern Plains taken from the Tenth Census of the US, 1880.

State/territory	Cattle 1860	Cattle 1880
Kansas	93,455	1,533,133
Nebraska	37,197	1,113,247
Colorado	none	791,492
Wyoming	none	521,213
Montana	none	428,279
Dakota	none	140,815

What was the 'open range'?

The ranches on the Great Plains often covered hundreds of thousands of hectares. The cattle roamed freely over them to graze on the grass. Each head of cattle was branded to show which ranch it belonged to. Each rancher needed a huge area to graze his cattle. However, no rancher could ever afford to buy all the land over which his animals grazed. The land was not, in fact, owned by anyone. It was unfenced: it was the 'open range'. Each rancher had his 'range rights' on the land. This included the right to reserve a stream or water hole for his cattle, together with the land which ran back to the next 'divide' which separated his watering place from the next one. Water supplies were important and ranchers competed fiercely to take over land near rivers and streams. If this was not possible, they dug wells.

Source 3

Examples of brandmarks. To show which cattle belonged to which ranch, cowboys burned brandmarks into the rumps or shoulders of the cattle.

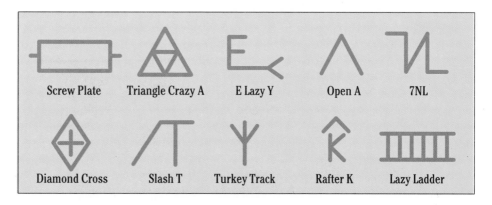

Screw Plate Triangle Crazy A E Lazy Y Open A 7NL

Diamond Cross Slash T Turkey Track Rafter K Lazy Ladder

Now that the cattle were raised on the Great Plains, ranchers began building themselves permanent living quarters. They built bunkhouses and living quarters for their cowboys. They built stables for their horses and barns for storing fodder, harnesses, bridles and saddles. People were, at last, beginning to settle on the Great Plains.

Questions

1 **a** Read Source 1. Why would a rancher need running water and timber?
   b It appears that the rancher wanted to get as far away as possible from farmers. Why was this?

2 The figures in Source 2 sum up the huge expansion of cattle rearing on the Great Plains. Use the information and sources in this unit to help you explain why this expansion took place.

Cowboys

Source 1
'In without knocking' by Charles Russell, 1909. Charles Russell worked on ranches between 1880 and 1892. This painting shows high-spirited cowboys at the end of a drive.

These pictures, both painted by men who had lived in the West, give very different impressions of a cowboy's life. Many cowboys were ex-Confederate soldiers. Some were black ex-slaves from the southern states. Others were restless young men from farming lands who wanted a life with more adventure than farming could offer. Was the job as attractive and romantic as the stories and the films make out? Or was it just tiring and dirty and boring?

What was the life of a cowboy really like?

The cowboy's job was to look after the herds of cattle on the range. He rode the range for most of the year rounding up cattle and branding them. He rode round the boundaries of the range to make sure that no one took over these distant parts. This was called 'riding the line'. Then he had to drive the cattle to market. In the days of the long drives from Texas to rail-heads like Sedalia or Abilene, the cowboys spent most of their time on the trail. When ranching on the Great Plains began to take over from the long drives, cowboys had a slightly more comfortable life. They had bunkhouses in which to sleep, cookhouses where their food was prepared and somewhere to shelter. However, they still had to ride the line and drive the cattle to market in all weathers. Here George Duffield describes some of the problems.

Source 2

This painting is called 'On the trail'. It was painted by Frederic Remington who worked on a sheep farm in Kansas and travelled widely in the West.

Source 3

This is from the diary of George Duffield. He drove a herd of 1,000 Longhorns from Southern Texas to Iowa in 1866.

* **provisions** Food and drink.
* **beeves** Cattle.

May 8   Rain pouring down in torrents. Ran my horse into a ditch and got my knee badly sprained.

May 14   Brazoz River. Swam our cattle and horses and built raft and rafted our provisions* and blankets and so on over. Swam river with rope and then hauled wagon over. Lost most of our camp kettles, coffee pots, cups, etc.

June 1   Stampede last night among six droves and a general mix up and loss of beeves*. Hunt cattle again. Men all tired and want to leave.

June 2   Hard rain and wind storm. Beeves ran and I had to be on horseback all night. Awful night. Almost starved not having had a bite to eat for 60 hours. Go to camp about 12.00. Tired.

June 19   Arkansas River. Fifteen Indians came to herd and tried to take some beeves. Would not let them. One drew his knife and I my revolver. Made them leave but fear they have gone for others.

Theodore Roosevelt was President of the United States 1901–9. When he was a young man he worked for some years as a cowboy. In 1896 he wrote a book about his experiences:

Source 4

T. Roosevelt, *Ranch Life and the Hunting Trail*, 1896.

* **mired in** Sunk in mud.
* **quagmire** Wet, boggy ground.
* **tenacious** Clinging.

During the early spring months before the round-up begins, the chief work is in hauling out mired in* cows and steers. As long as everything is frozen solid there is, of course, no danger from miring; but when the thaw comes along towards the beginning of March the frost goes out of the soil, the ground round every little alkali-spring changes into a trembling quagmire*, and deep holes of slimy, tenacious* mud from the bottom of the gullies. The cattle which have had to live on snow for three or four months, are very eager for water, and are weak and in poor condition. They rush heedlessly into any pool and stand there, drinking gallons of icy water and sinking steadily into the mud.

Life for cowboys living and working on ranches on the Great Plains brought additional problems.

Source 5

J. Evetts Haley, *X I T Ranch of Texas and the Early Days of the Llano Estacado*, 1953.

Extract from the Rules of the X I T Ranch, 1888.

No. 11 No employee of the Company is permitted to carry on or about his person or saddlebags any pistol, dagger, knuckles, bowie knife or any other similar instruments for the purpose of offense or defense.

No. 12 Card playing and gambling of every description is strictly forbidden on the ranch.

No. 15 Employees are strictly forbidden the use of vinous, malt, spiritous or intoxicating liquors during their time of service with the Company.

Source 6

A still from the film *Wyatt Earp* made in 1992.

Questions

1 What can you learn from Sources 1–5 about:
   a the weather
   b difficult ground
   c Indians
   d cattle?

2 Look at Sources 1 and 2. What different impressions do they give about the life of a cowboy? Use the information and sources in this section to explain which painting you think is the more accurate.

3 Look at Source 6 which is a still from a film. Use your knowledge of the way of life of cowboys to explain what is accurate and what is inaccurate in this picture. Why do you think the film makers didn't try to make their image of the cowboy more accurate?

The end of the open range

Source 1

Charles Russell's painting 'Waiting for the chinook: last of 5000?' shows a scene from the 1886–87 winter, when hopes of the warm, dry chinook wind were far away. It was painted in 1887.

If the Great Plains were to go on supporting vast numbers of cattle, they needed to grow good, sweet grass. This meant good weather: rain and sun at the right times. However, the vast herds grazing over the Great Plains once cattle ranching began meant that, even with good weather, the grass was not always going to be good when the cattle needed it to be. Some cattlemen began thinking the unthinkable: they would fence their land to keep their neighbours' cattle out.

Falling profits

By 1882 profits from cattle ranching were beginning to fall. Cattle fetched lower and lower prices at the Chicago stockyards. There was simply too much meat about. Some ranchers sold up, and the price of cattle fell still further.

The winter of 1886–87

The cold, blustery winter of 1885–86 hit cattle and cattlemen hard. The summer that followed in 1886 was so hot and dry that it withered the grass and dried up the streams. Ranchers panicked and many sold their herds. The winter that followed in 1886–87 was the worst in living memory. Temperatures fell as low as –68°. Cattle could not reach the grass through the deep snow. The Longhorns, usually so hardy, died in their thousands.

Barbed wire

The cattlemen realised that something had to be done. Grass and cattle had to be balanced, and this meant fencing the open range. There were, however, two major problems in fencing off land successfully. The fencing had to be sturdy enough to keep one rancher's cattle in and another's out. The land that was fenced in had to have a reliable water supply.

In 1874 Joseph Gliddon of Illinois produced a successful pattern for barbed wire. There had been many attempts to make good barbed wire before Gliddon's success, but none took off as his did. In 1880 alone, 36,600 tonnes were made and sold. Some people realised how important barbed wire was to become.

Source 2

W. S. James, *Cowboy Life in Texas*, 1893.

> When I saw a barbed wire machine at work manufacturing it and was told that there were thousands of them at the same work, I went home and told the boys they might just as well put up their cutters and quit splitting rails and use barbed wire instead.

The farmers (see Unit 6, page 86) were the first to make use of barbed wire. They fenced off their holdings on the Great Plains and the cattlemen hated them for it. Fence-cutting wars broke out in places like Texas and Wyoming, where farmers' and cattlemen's demands on land met and clashed. In the end, though, the cattlemen realised that if they were to survive they too had to use barbed wire.

Water

Ranchers used wind pumps to solve the water problem. Some pumps (see page 85) were large and fixed. They pumped water from deep in the ground. Others were portable. This meant that ranchers could reach water wherever the herds were pastured. Cattlemen could now fence off their land even if there was no running water at all.

Once the range was fenced, cowboys no longer had to 'ride the line' or round up and brand cattle. Cowboys were still there, but their jobs had changed. They put up and repaired fences, moved herds from one pasture to another, made hay which they fed to the herds when the grass was poor and drove the cattle to market.

Questions

1 **a** Explain what the following had to do with the ending of the open range:
      (i)   the weather
      (ii) falling profits
      (iii) barbed wire
      (iv   water pumps.
   b Was any one of these reasons any more important than the others? Explain your answer.

Unit 5 Review

Questions

1 How were the Great Plains used by cattlemen and cowboys between 1837 and 1895? Draw a timeline to show what happened.

2 Use the information and sources in this unit to explain why the railroads were so important to the cattlemen and cowboys.

3 How did the life and work of the cowboys change between 1837 and 1895? Copy the grid below and use the information and sources in this unit to fill it in.

	First trails	Long drives	Ranching	The fenced range
What work did they do? What special skills did they need? Where did they live? How did they live?				

Milt Hinkle, in *True West Magazine*, No 47, October 1961, Western Publications Inc.

As I muse over my past life it occurs to me that possibly more has been written about the American cowboy, more has been said, more moving pictures made of and about him, than any other character in American history. I am proud to have been one of those early day cowboys. He is the most romantic, glamorised and most misunderstood figure ever to ride across the pages of our history.

4 a What can you find out about Milt Hinckle from this source?
   b What evidence can you find in this unit to support Milt Hinckle when he says that cowboys have been romanticised and glamourised?
   c Why do you think Milt Hinckle says that the cowboy is 'misunderstood'?

Unit 6 · The homesteaders

The cattlemen and cowboys made good use of the rich grasses on the Great Plains. They built up large and profitable ranches. They adapted themselves and their way of life to the Great Plains. They did not try to change the land or what was growing there. It was the homesteaders who determinedly battled against tremendous odds to tame the Great Plains and turn them into rich farmlands.

Some of the people who came to the Great Plains were freed slaves from the southern states. Others were immigrants from Europe trying to get away from poverty, unemployment and, sometimes, religious persecution. By far the largest group, however, were Americans from the states east of the Mississippi River.

What drove the homesteaders to try to settle and farm on the Great Plains? The early pioneers (pages 39–44) saw the Great Plains as a terrible barrier which had to be crossed in order to reach the fertile farmlands of Oregon and California. However, by the 1860s most of the land there had been settled and was very expensive to buy. For ordinary men and women in search of land, adventure and a new start in life, the Great Plains offered them their only chance.

Help for settlers on the Great Plains

What did the government do to help?

The US government (see page 34) wanted Americans to settle on the Great Plains. To encourage them to do this, it tried to make sure of two things. It tried to make it easy for settlers to own the land on which they settled, and it tried to keep law and order on the Great Plains.

'Public domain'
All the land opened for settlement in the West was 'public domain'. This meant that it belonged to no one and could be settled by anyone. The US government decided to change this. It tried to make sure that as much land as possible had an owner. It had the land surveyed and divided into areas of 9.6 km², called townships. Each township was divided up into sections of one square mile (640 acres or 259 hectares). The government wanted families to buy up a section each, and offered the sections for sale at $1 per acre. However, it soon became clear that very few families could afford to buy a section in a township. Land speculators moved in. They bought all the land they could at $1 an acre, and sold it on at a higher price to those settlers who could afford to pay. This was not at all what the government had intended to happen.

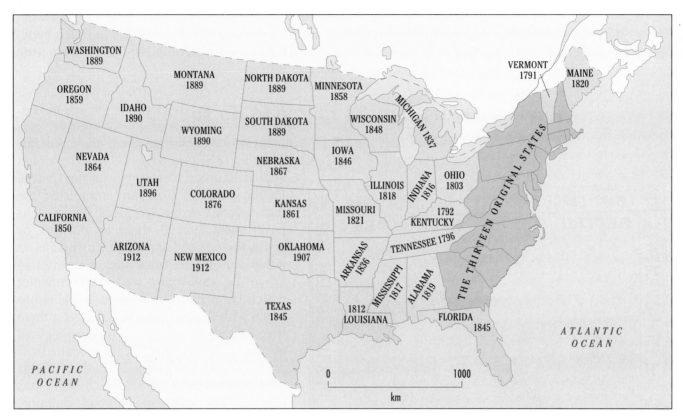

States of the USA with dates of their admission to the Union.

Homestead Act, 1862

In order to try to stop land speculation, Congress passed the Homestead Act in 1862. Settlers could claim a quarter-section of land to live on and to farm. This claim had to be entered in an official land register. After five years the settler could pay $30 and get a certificate of ownership. In other words, public land was virtually free. Source 2 comes from the Act and explains how this was to happen.

Taken from *An Act to Secure Homesteads to Actual Settlers on the Public Domain*, May 20 1862.

No certificate shall be given until the expiration of five years from the date of entry; and if, at the end of such time, the person making such entry or his widow or heirs, shall prove by two truthful witnesses that he, she or they have resided upon or cultivated the same for five years, and that he has borne true allegiance to the Government of the United States, then, in such case, he, she or they, if at that time a citizen of the United States, shall be entitled to a patent stating that they own the land.

The Civil War 1861–65

Thousands of people were persuaded to tackle the life of the homesteader as an indirect result of government action. A fierce and bitter civil war had been fought in America between 1861 and 1865. On one side were the slave-owning southern states, the Confederate states. They were fighting for the right to manage their own affairs and to opt out of the Union of states if they wished. On the other side were the industrial northern states, generally opposed to slavery, and determined that all the states within

America should hold fast together in one Union. The northern states won. Thousands of former negro slaves fled the southern states to find a better life on the Great Plains. With them went hundreds of ex-soldiers from both Confederate and Union armies.

What did the railroads do to help?

It was not only the US government which encouraged and made possible the settlement of the Great Plains. In 1869 (see pages 58–61) the Union Pacific Railroad Company and the Central Pacific Railroad Company completed the first railroad across the Great Plains. The government helped them to do this by giving the railroad companies townships on either side of the track they were putting down. By 1893 there were six companies which connected the Mississippi–Missouri rivers with the Pacific coast. Between them they owned about 155 million acres of land on the Great Plains. In order to make their railroads pay, the companies had to sell this land. Money from the sale of the land was used to finance more railroad building. Furthermore, the sale of land would, the companies hoped, attract more passengers and freight as more people would travel west and live and work there.

The railroad companies began a massive advertising campaign, not only in America but also in the whole of northern Europe. Pamphlets and posters flooded Sweden, Norway, Denmark, Holland, Germany, France and Britain. Thousand of men and women were attracted by the promise of cheap land. They crossed the Atlantic, determined to make a good life for themselves and their families on the Great Plains.

Source 3

A railroad advertisement about the sale of land, 1875.

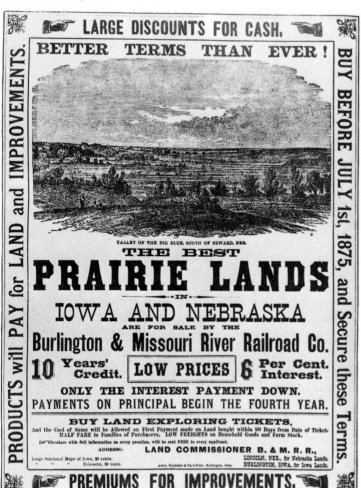

Questions

1   What does the Homestead Act (1862) show about the way in which the US government wanted the West settled?

2   How did the railroad companies profit from people wanting to settle on the Great Plains?

3   What sorts of people became homesteaders?

Homesteaders settle on the Great Plains

The first people to decide to try to live on the Plains faced enormous problems: how to live on the Plains and how to farm them. They solved these problems in different ways and with different degrees of success. Some stayed and became prosperous farmers; other quit altogether. In between came the thousands who struggled on, convincing themselves that, tomorrow, things would be better.

How did the homesteaders get to the Plains?

Many homesteaders travelled to their new lands by train (see pages 58–61). Others used the old way of travel: by wagon. Some used a combination of train and wagon. In Source 1, Hamlin Garland explains how his family got there:

Source 1

Hamlin Garland, *A Son of the Middle Border*, Macmillan

Source 2

The 'modern ship of the plains'. travelling on an emigrant train, 1886. Published in the magazine *Harpers Weekly*, November 1886.

> Each mile took us farther and farther into the unsettled prairie until in the afternoon of the second day, we came to a meadow so wide that its western rim touched the sky without revealing a sign of man's habitation other than the road on which we travelled. The plain was covered with grass as tall as ripe wheat and when my father stopped his team of horses pulling the wagon, and came back to us and said 'Well children, here we are on the Big Prairie', we looked around us with awe.

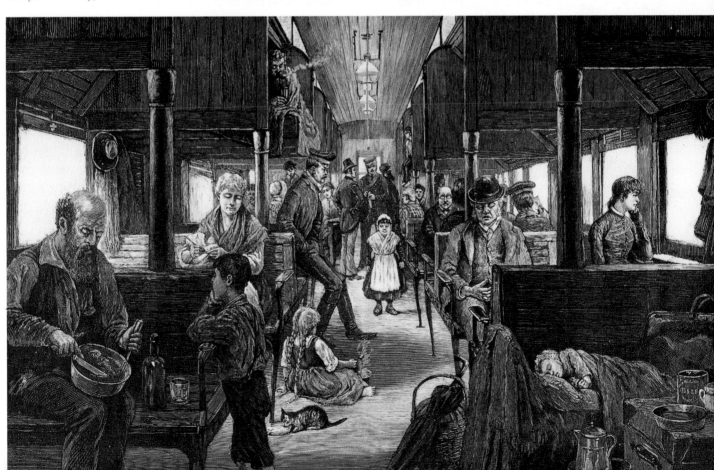

How did the homesteaders build houses for themselves?

No matter how the settlers got to the Plains, once a claim was staked and registered, all families faced the same problem: how to build a house. Obviously the homesteaders had to build with the raw materials which they had on their own land. Most settlers, however, lived far from the woods on the fringes of the Plains. They lived way out on the open Plain, with no trees to be seen, and only the endlessly waving grass for miles and miles. Houses could not be built from grass, but what else was there? There was the solid earth – and this is what the homesteaders used. First by hand, and later with specially-built ploughs, they cut blocks of earth (sods) which they used as building bricks. Because of this, the homesteaders were nicknamed 'sodbusters'.

Sod houses were solid and strong. They had to withstand gales and storms, drought and blistering heat, grasshoppers and prairie fires. They also had to house men, women and children, and keep them warm enough and well enough so that they could work hard enough to make a living from the prairie land outside.

It took about an acre (0.4 hectares) of land to provide enough sods to build an average sod house on the Great Plains. Homesteaders used the sods as bricks to build the house walls, which were sometimes as much as a metre thick. They left spaces for the windows and doors, and roofed the house with grass and more sods. Once the house was built, the homesteaders plastered it on the outside with masses of clay-like mud. When it set hard the mud made the house more or less watertight.

Source 3

The sod house of J. C. Cram and his family in Loup County, Nebraska, 1886.

What work did women do on the Great Plains?

It was an achievement to build a house out of sods of earth for yourself and your family. It was even more of an achievement to live in a sod house successfully and to manage day-to-day living so that your family was warm, fed, clothed, clean and healthy. This, inevitably, was the responsibility of the women.

Fuel and food

Every homesteader needed fuel. Without fuel the homesteader family would be cold, hungry and dirty. There were hardly any trees on the Great Plains, and so no wood to burn. The sod-buster's wife therefore collected barrow-loads of dried cow and buffalo dung which burned well, and had fuel in plenty. These 'cow-chips', however, burned very quickly and stoves had to be stoked up very frequently. Charlie O'Kieffe remembers watching his mother bake biscuits:

Source 4

C. O'Kieffe, *Western Story: The Recollections of C. O'Kieffe*, 1960.

Stoke the stove, get out the flour sack, stoke the stove, wash your hands, mix the dough, stoke the stove, wash your hands, cut out the biscuits with the top of the baking powder can, stoke the stove, wash your hands, put the pan of biscuits in the oven, keep on stoking the stove until the biscuits are done.

Meals were often monotonous and very boring. One schoolteacher, Mollie Sanford, living with a family of sod-busters, wrote:

Source 5

M. Sandford, *Journal of Mollie D. Sandford* 1857–66, 1959.

For breakfast we had corn bread, salt pork and black coffee. For dinner, greens, wild ones at that, boiled pork and cold corn bread washed down with 'beverage'. The 'beverage' was put upon the table in a wooden pail and dished out in tin cups. When asked if I would have some I said 'Yes', thinking it was cider, but found out it was vinegar and brown sugar and warm creek water.

Dirt and disease

People and clothes had to be kept clean, and so did houses. Spiders, fleas and all kinds of insects lived in the earth walls and floors of sod houses. Even with modern detergents and vacuum cleaners it would have been impossible to keep such a house really clean. The sod-buster's wife had an uncertain water supply, little soap and rags, and brushes made from twigs. She fought an unending battle against dirt and disease. All the women had well-tried remedies for illness which they adapted to life on the Great Plains. For example, they put warm manure on a snake bite; poured urine into an ear that was aching; wrapped a cobweb around a cut and persuaded someone with measles to eat a well-roasted mouse. Source 6 describes how Dr Barns' wife got rid of bed bugs.

Source 6

G. C. Barns, *The Sod House*, 1970.

My wife became unhappy when she saw bed bugs racing up the walls. She had a good, thick whitewash made and plastered the walls and got rid of the bed bugs.

Pregnancy and childbirth

When women gave birth on the Great Plains there were no maternity hospitals or community midwives to help them. Charlie O'Kieffe tells us:

Source 7

C. O'Kieffe, *Western Story: The Recollections of C O'Kieffe*, 1960.

> According to what I've been told, Mother herded cattle all day long in the broiling sun. The next morning, around 2.00 a.m., I was born. No doctor, no nurse, no midwife, just Mother and God; and two days later she was up and doing her regular housework.

Source 8

S. Magoffin, *Down the Santa Fe Trail into Mexico*, 1926.

> I do think a pregnant woman has a hard time of it. Some sickness all the time, heart-burn, headache, cramp, etc., after all this thing of marrying is not what it is cracked up to be.

Teachers and teaching

Not all the women who travelled on to the Great Plains were married. In 1859 the *Lynne County Herald* [Kansas] printed an advertisement for 'One hundred schoolmarms, who will pledge themselves not to get married within three years.'

Schoolteachers were needed to teach the children living on the Great Plains and in the growing townships. The pay was usually low, and most lived with the families of the children they taught. The 'schoolmarm' did not have to struggle in the same way as the homesteader's wife, but she had to struggle against prejudice and ignorance, and she had to work in appalling conditions.

Source 9

A 'schoolmarm' surrounded by her pupils, Custer County, Nebraska 1889.

Source 10

R. Holt, 'The Pioneer Teacher' in *Sheep and Goat Raiser*, 1955.

When she asked each child to bring his own drinking cup, a delegation of school directors appeared demanding to know the reason for such nonsense. She won the argument and proceeded to other matters. 'There was not the slightest sign of a toilet. When I told the directors that I could not teach if they did not build one, one of them remarked "Now you see what comes of hiring someone from the Outside. Never had any trouble before, plenty of trees to get behind." '

Some 'schoolmarms' were tough in a different way. The women 'school-marms', by insisting on certain standards of behaviour and speech, did a great deal to make the West a more civilised place.

Indians

Sometimes the women homesteaders coped alone with Indians, often with surprising results.

Source 11

Dee Brown, *The Gentle Tamers*, 1958.

A warrior and a small band visited a tent camp, and seeing bright coloured quilts and shiny utensils all about and no one near but a few 'white squaws', he decided to help himself. One of the 'white squaws', however, began defending her possessions with a heavy tent pole. 'She laid about, right and left, over heads, shoulders and backs until she put them to flight.' The next day the warrior returned, apologised for his conduct, and offered the woman's husband $500 for her. He was quite disappointed to learn she was not for sale.

Source 12

H. Horn, *The Pioneers*, 1974.

The two women saw the Cheyenne warriors approaching across the prairie. Mrs Kine plunged into the creek at a point where she was hidden by some brush overhanging the bank, and held her baby high to keep it from drowning. But Mrs Alardice, paralyzed with fear, collapsed in a faint surrounded by her four quaking children. The Cheyennes shot the three oldest boys, killing two of them. They then galloped off with Mrs Alardice and her youngest child. The baby cried so lustily that the Indians became enraged, choked it to death and left the body beside the trail. The mother later died.

Questions

1 What different problems were faced by (i) men and (ii) women in settling the Great Plains? How did women set about dealing with these problems?

2 Read Sources 11 and 12 again.
 a What do they tell us about the attitudes of Indians toward white settlers?
 b What do they tell us about the attitudes of white people toward Indians?

Farming: the problems

Most of the people who set up as homesteaders in the West had had experience of farming in the south and east of America or in Europe. However, the soil and climate on the Great Plains were different from anything they had experienced before. No one had ever farmed the Great Plains. No one knew which crops to grow or how best to prepare the land. All the homesteaders could do was to use the methods which they knew worked elsewhere.

What were the problems?

Ploughing and sowing

Before crops could be grown, homesteaders had to plough the ground so that seed could be planted. The Great Plains had never before been ploughed. The grasses which grew there had roots which formed a dense tangled mass at least 10 cm thick. The cast iron ploughs which many homesteaders brought with them bent and buckled under the strain and had to be repaired constantly. Making the land productive was a slow and back-breaking job.

Water

An average of 38 cm of rain fell in a normal year on the Great Plains. This was just not enough for agriculture. To make matters worse, it fell at the wrong time: in the summer when the sun and hot winds dried up what moisture there was in the soil. Crops simply would not grow well, and sometimes did not grow at all. A series of dreadful droughts hit Kansas and Nebraska. No rain fell between January 1859 and November 1860. A regular supply of water was clearly essential.

Source 1

An ox-drawn plough breaks the sod on a Kansas farm. This drawing appeared in *Harper's Weekly* in May 1868.

The 'old' solutions would have been to irrigate or dig a well. On the Great Plains irrigation was impossible because there were no lakes or rivers from which to dig drainage ditches. Many farmers did dig wells, but this was an uncertain and expensive business. In any case, homesteaders with wells of their own rarely had enough water to irrigate their crops properly. Everyone went short as the precious water was shared between those who needed it.

Land holdings

The size of a homesteader's holding was clearly important. It had to be large enough to support himself and his family, and small enough for him to work himself or with family help. The government allocation (see page 74) of 160 acres could not yield enough to support the average homesteader and his family.

Crops

At first homesteaders planted the crops they knew best. They planted maize and soft winter and spring wheats. These crops did not do well on the Great Plains, with their low rainfall, scorching hot summers and extremely cold winters. In order to make farming a profitable business, farmers have to grow crops which will fetch a good price. It was the same for the homesteader, except that he had first to find a crop which he could grow successfully.

Source 2

A maize field and sod house in Nebraska in the 1880s.

Fencing

Homesteaders needed to fence their land so as to make a clear boundary between their claim and the claims of their neighbours. They also needed to stop the ranchers' cattle from straying onto their claim and destroying the crops they were trying to grow. However, they did not have timber with which to build fences, and hedging plants would not grow quickly enough, even if they survived.

Devastation: fire and grasshoppers

Homesteaders had to cope with many hazards, but the most terrifying of these was fire. In the summer and autumn, when the prairie grasslands were bone dry, the merest spark could set off a fire which ran wild. Homesteaders could beat out small fires. However, once fire got a hold, all the homesteader and his family could do was to hide inside their sod house while their crops were destroyed and the fire burnt itself out.

Devastation came, too, from another source and was every bit as deadly. Between 1874 and 1877, Rocky Mountain locusts (grasshoppers) swarmed through the prairies devouring everything in their way. It seemed there was nothing they wouldn't eat: crops and tree bark, leather boots and buckets, wooden door frames – even washing. Here, Jennie Flint explains why her family is so desperate:

Source 3

Part of a letter from Jennie Flint of Minnesota to Governor Davies, asking for help.

> We have no money nor nothing to sell to get any clothes as the grasshoppers destroyed all of our crop.

Clearly most homesteaders were determined to survive on the Great Plains. However, if they were to do more than simply survive, they needed to find new ways of farming. New inventions, discoveries or techniques were needed if the homesteaders were to succeed and prosper.

Question

1   The homesteaders faced many problems as they struggled to make a living by farming the Great Plains.
   a Make a list of the problems.
   b Which problem (or problems) were short-term and had to be solved immediately?
   c Which problem (or problems) were long-term and had to be solved if they were to stay on the Great Plains for years and make a success of farming there?

Farming: the solutions

The women adapted very quickly to living in a sod house. The men took longer to change their old ways of farming. This was partly because it took a long time for them to realise that the old methods simply were not suitable. It takes many months to realise that a crop is not growing properly, and several years to realise that one bad year is not an accident but that all years will be bad.

How were the problems solved?

Machinery

Gradually the factories in the east of the United States began to mass produce farm machinery. Mechanical reapers, binders and threshers became cheaper. Furthermore, mass-produced machinery came with spare parts and could be easily repaired out on the Great Plains if something went wrong. From the mid-1880s farm machinery helped the homesteader cultivate more land without needing more men. A man with a sickle and flail could harvest 7.5 acres (3 hectares) of wheat in the same time that a man with a mechanical reaper could harvest 100 acres (40.5 hectares).

Wind pumps

Farmers could not always hold on to the land they staked out on the dry and arid plains. They gave up because they could not find water – or because they could not find enough water. There was always water below the surface soil, but sometimes it was a very long way below. The homesteaders needed some mechanical means of raising water to the surface which was cheap to build and run, and which could produce water in a steady flow. Both cattlemen and railroad builders used wind pumps, and these were soon quickly adapted to meet the needs of the farmer. First a high-powered drill had to be used to get down to the water, which was sometimes several hundred metres beneath the surface. Then a wind pump was built to raise the water to the surface and to get it to where it was needed. It was hardly surprising that from the middle of the 1880s a wind pump dominated most of the homesteads on the Great Plains.

Source 1

A wind pump on a farm in Custer County, Nebraska, 1888.

Barbed wire

Barbed wire meant that the homesteaders could fence their land quickly, efficiently and cheaply. They could plant crops knowing that herds of cattle would not stray on to their land and trample and eat the growing plants. They could experiment with animal breeding, knowing that stray bulls would not mate with their stock. However, in using barbed wire to protect their own livelihood, the homesteaders destroyed that of other people. Barbed wire threatened the open range (see pages 71–72) and the cattlemen and cowboys were not going to give up their way of life easily.

Railroads

Wind pumps and drill, barbed wire and mechanical reapers, threshers and binders were all essential to the prosperity of the farmer on the Great Plains. However, they were not manufactured on the Plains. The homesteaders were only able to benefit from them because of the railroad. The railroads brought ploughs and reapers, furniture and fabrics, steam traction engines and barbed wire to the homesteaders. They also made it possible for the homesteaders to sell their crops in markets far from the Great Plains.

Legislation

The US government finally realised that 160 acres of land was not enough for successful farming on the Great Plains. In 1873 they passed the Timber and Culture Act, which allowed a homesteader to claim a further 160 acres provided he promised to plant trees on half of it. This Act really did mean that the ordinary homesteader, who could not afford to buy land, was able to make a reasonable living.

New techniques and crops

Dry farming was a technique learned by the homesteaders. It was a method which tried to keep the moisture in the soil by ploughing the ground every time it rained. This ploughing left a layer of fine dust on the moist soil which stopped the moisture evaporating. In this way homesteaders conserved water and grew better crops.

The soft wheats which the early homesteaders had sown did not do well. This was largely because of the very hard winters and the hot, dry summers of the Great Plains. In 1874 a group of Russian migrants arrived on the Great Plains. They brought with them 'Turkey Red' which was a variety of wheat that grew well in the extremes of the Russian climate. By 1881 the homesteaders had worked out a way of grinding this new, hard wheat. Growing Turkey Red wheat, using the dry farming method, was beginning to be very profitable indeed.

By itself, each of these inventions, discoveries and developments would not have ensured success for the homesteader. Some were more important than others. Some were more important than others at different times and in different places and to different people. What is vital is that they all came together at the right time to enable the homesteaders, by 1890, to control the Great Plains. The homesteaders were no longer forced to change their lives to adapt to the Great Plains. They were able to force the Great Plains to become rich, fertile farmlands beyond the wildest imagining of the early pioneers.

Were all homesteaders successful on the Great Plains?

Just as the homesteaders had very different experiences when they were getting started, so they differed in whether or not they made a success of their lives on the Great Plains. This was due to a number of factors, for example, the skills they brought with them, the land on which they staked their claim, their own determination, their health and sheer good or bad luck. These three sources describe some very different experiences.

Source 2

From a journal called *Atlantic Monthly*, 1893.

Life, shut up in the little wooden farmhouses, cannot be very cheerful. A drive to the nearest town is almost the only diversion. There the farmers and their wives gather in the stores and manage to enjoy a little sociability. There are few social events in the life of these prairie farmers to enliven the monotony of the long winter evenings; no singing schools, spelling schools, debating clubs or church gatherings. Neighbourly calls are infrequent because of the long distances which separate farmhouses.

Source 3

C. G. Barns, *The Sod House*, 1970. C. G. Barns was a young doctor on the Great Plains in 1878.

Our neighbourhood people were a fine class of people. Social gatherings were common as were the lunches of fried chicken, cake and delicacies. The sod schoolhouse had given way to a small frame building. This house became the public hall for all entertainments, social gatherings, Sunday School and religious services.

Source 4

Part of a report in a Kansas newspaper, *The Gazette*, 1895.

There came through yesterday two old-fashioned mover wagons headed east, four horses, very poor and very tired, and one sad-eyed dog. A few farm implements of the simpler sort were loaded in the wagon. For ten years they had been fighting the elements. They have tossed through hot nights, wild with worry, and have arisen only to find their worse nightmares grazing in reality on the brown stubble in front of their sun-warped doors. They had such high hopes when they went out.

Questions

1   Would it be true to say that, by 1895, the homesteaders' problems had been solved? Use the information and sources in this unit in your answer.

2   Use your knowledge of the ways in which the Great Plains were settled to explain how both Sources 2 and 3 could be correct.

3   By the 1890s the Great Plains had become prosperous farmlands. Does this mean that Source 4 must be unreliable?

Questions

1   The US government was involved in helping to make the settlement of the Great Plains possible. Copy the grid below. For each government action, explain how that action helped the homesteaders settle the Great Plains.

Government action	How it helped the homesteaders settle the Great Plains
The Homestead Act, 1862 Federal Territories Grants of land to railroad companies The Civil War Timber and Culture Act, 1873	

2   How was the US government helping the American people fulfil their 'manifest destiny'? Look back to Unit 3 to remind yourself what this was.

3   Read these two sources carefully:

Emerson Hough, *The Passing of the Frontier*, 1921.

* **gaunt** Very thin.
* **brethren** Brothers.

> The chief figure of the American West is not the long haired, fringed legging man riding a rawboned pony, but the gaunt* and sad-faced woman sitting on the front seat of the wagon, following her lord wherever he might lead. That was America, my brethren*! There was the seed of America's wealth.

Walter P. Webb, *The Great Plains*, 1931.

> The Great Plains in the early period was strictly a man's country. There was a zest to the life, adventure in the air, freedom from restraint; men developed a hardihood which made them insensible to the hardships and lack of refinements. But what of the women? Most of the evidence, such as it is, reveals that the Plains repelled the women as they attracted the men. There was too much of the unknown, too few of the things they loved. If we could get at the truth we should doubtless find that many a family was stopped on the edge of the timber by women who refused to go further. Who can tell us how the Great Plains affected women, and why?

Use what you know about the settlement of the Great Plains to explain whether you agree with the opinions of Emerson Hough or Walter P. Webb.

Unit 7 · Law and order

Keeping law and order in the West was a problem in those areas which were growing, but had not long been organised. It took time to set up effective government in new territories (see pages 34 and 56) This was especially true when the territories covered vast areas of land, and were far away from fully organised states like California and the states east of the Mississippi. Even when the system had been set up, it did not always work properly. Men who were supposed to keep law and order were not always honest. Criminals were often able to outwit even honest lawmen.

Problems of law and order in the mining regions

There were two main gold rushes in the West: in 1848–99 and 1858–89 (see pages 54–56). In the first rush, thousands of unmarried men flooded into California. Ten years later it was the turn of the mountain areas (which were to become Colorado and Nevada). Most of the early miners were law abiding. Some, however, were violent and disruptive. The main difficulties in the mining areas were to do with gold and claims to land. There were no laws to authorise mining in these areas, or to give legal ownership to those who claimed land. Miners were, therefore, trespassing on public domain (see page 74). This led to claim jumping, when men simply seized land which had been claimed by other miners. Anger and violence followed. Gold attracted not only the honest miner, but also the swindler, the robber and the con-man.

Miners' courts and Vigilance Committees

With the city of Washington and the federal law far away, miners took the law into their own hands. They set up their own miners' courts to hand out rough justice. Sometimes, however, the miners' courts could not cope. Maybe there was too much violence; maybe there was too much lying and too much intrigue; maybe those accused and found guilty simply would not accept the verdict of the court. Ordinary citizens were often so concerned that they set up Vigilance Committees. These Vigilance Committees took the law into their own hands. They held instant trials, after which many a condemned man would be seen hanging from a nearby tree, guilty or not.

Vigilantes in Bannack, Montana

Source 1

G. Stuart, *Forty Years on the Frontier*, Vol. 1,

These were dark days in Bannack; there was no safety for life or property only so far as each individual could, with his trusty rifle, protect his own. The respectable citizens far outnumbered the desperadoes, but having come from all corners of the earth, they were unacquainted and did not know whom to trust. On the other hand, the 'Roughs' were organised and under the able leadership of that accompliced villain, Henry Plummer. At times it would seem that they had the upper hand and would run affairs to suit themselves.

What happened in Bannack was typical of what happened in many mining areas. The people of Bannack were being terrorised by a gang of about 100 road agents (highwaymen) They robbed miners and other travellers. They were a well-organised gang, and even wore special knots in their ties so that they could recognise each other. It gradually became clear that the man who had been elected sheriff in Bannack, Henry Plummer, a well-respected member of the community, was the leader of this gang. A Vigilance Committee was set up, and one of the gang confessed all. Plummer tried to escape but was caught and hanged by the vigilantes in 1864.

Did the vigilantes do more harm than good?

It would seem that vigilante groups were necessary in places like Bannack where they cleared the mining areas of individuals and gangs who terrorised honest citizens. Source 2 explains that in some circumstances the activities of Vigilance Committees could be considered legal.

Source 2

Professor D. J. Dimsdale, *The Vigilantes of Montana*, 1865.

Justice and protection from wrong to person and to property are the birthright of every American citizen. These must be provided by constitutional law whenever provision can be made for its enforcement. But when justice is powerless as well as blind 'self preservation is the first law of nature'.

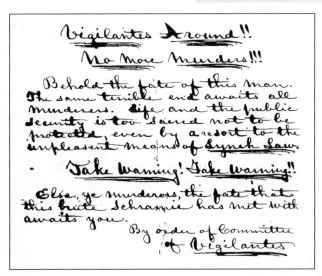

However, people in the towns and camps sometimes feared the vigilantes themselves. The 'trials' which the vigilantes held were often too hasty for any real justice to be done, especially when it was clear what people wanted the verdict to be. There was no appeal from the verdict, either. It was all too easy to execute someone who had got on the wrong side of an influential citizen.

Source 3

A vigilante warning found pinned to the body of a man lynched for murder. Lynch law is punishment by the mob, without a proper legal trial.

Questions

1 Why did vigilante groups come into existence?

2 Would you agree with the statement 'Vigilante groups did more harm than good'? Use the sources and information in this section to explain your answer.

Gunslingers and gangs

Most of the legendary shoot-outs in the Wild West are set in the cow-towns of the mid-west, like Dodge City. There is no doubt that there were trigger-happy gangs and high-spirited cowboys in these towns. There were also bank and train robberies. Butch Cassidy and the Sundance Kid were not invented for the cinema! It is doubtful, however, whether it was all quite as glamorous or as violent as books and films would lead us to believe.

Source 1

R. A. Billington, *Westward Expansion*, 1967.

*ordinances Rules.

Ordinances* against carrying guns were in force in all the Cattle Towns; between 1870 and 1885 only forty-five men were killed (including sixteen by the police) and of these thirty-nine died of gun-shot wounds, not six-shooters. Only twice were as many as five men killed during a single year – in Ellsworth in 1873 and in Dodge City five years later. The 'shoot-out' glorified in 'western' stories and motion pictures was unheard of. In all the Cattle Towns only three men were executed for crime and one was lynched; not one of these was a cowboy and none convicted of gun fighting or a shooting affair.

Many gun-men crossed and re-crossed the boundary between what was legal and what was illegal. There was not always a lot of difference between a law-man like Wyatt Earp and a gunslinger like Jesse James. Wyatt Earp worked in Wichita, serving with the marshal and his assistants. He lasted for two years before he was arrested, fined and sacked for disturbing the peace.

Source 2

A poster offering a reward for the capture of Jesse James and his gang.

REWARD!
- DEAD OR ALIVE -

$5,000.⁰⁰ will be paid for the capture of the men who robbed the bank at

NORTHFIELD, MINN.

They are believed to be Jesse James and his Band, or the Youngers.

All officers are warned to use precaution in making arrest. These are the most desperate men in America.

Take no chances! Shoot to kill!!

J. H. McDonald, SHERIFF

Source 3

'The James Brothers' by N. C. Wyeth, showing Jesse James and his gang looking sinister and watchful.

Frank and Jesse James were widely known as bank robbers. They were born in Missouri, and after the Civil War they formed a band which specialised in train and bank robberies. They managed to escape the law until 1882. Jesse was shot in the back by Bob Ford, one of his own gang, who was after the reward promised in the poster (Source 3).

On the other hand, Thomas Smith, who became marshal of Abilene in 1870, managed to clean up the town within his first year. He was respected, feared and reasonably honest. Yet he was murdered later in 1870 whilst trying to make an arrest outside Abilene. Violence was never far below the surface.

Source 4

From a report in a newspaper, *The Wichita Tribune*, 1860.

I have been in a good many towns but Newton is the fastest one I have ever seen. Here you may see young girls, not over sixteen, drinking whisky, smoking cigars, cursing and swearing until one almost loses the respect they should have for the weaker sex. I heard one of their townsmen say that he didn't believe there were a dozen virtuous women in town. This speaks well for a town of 1,500 inhabitants. He further told me if I had any money that I would not be safe with it here. It is a common expression that they have a man every morning for breakfast.

Source 5

R. May, *The Story of the Wild West*, 1978.

In 1968, Robert Dykstra in his fine book *Cattle Towns* claimed that only forty-five killings took place between 1870 and 1885 and only a few were directly caused by gun-fights between lawmen and cowboys. But since then others have suggested that the total was far higher, especially in Dodge City and Newton.

That there was violence in the cow-towns is clear. Just how much violence there was is far from clear. However, it is certain that there was far more violence in the Range Wars between the cattlemen and the homesteaders than there ever was in the cow-towns between gunslingers and law-men.

Questions

1   In what ways do Sources 1, 4 and 5 *agree* about:
    a gun-fights
    b deaths
    c keeping law and order in the cow-towns?
    Does this mean that the things they agree about must be correct?

2   Source 3 was painted by N. C. Wyeth. What would the artist have had to check out to make sure his painting was accurate? What couldn't be checked, and so could be left to the artist's imagination?

The Johnson County War

Wyoming became a territory in 1868 and a state in 1890. It was well-organised and known to be peaceful. Yet in 1892, in a part of Wyoming called Johnson County, a fierce and bloody battle broke out between the two groups of inhabitants, the cattlemen and the farmers.

How did the cattlemen and farmers come to fight?

The land in Johnson County was good. Cattlemen set up ranches there, and, later, homesteaders flooded in. The cattlemen were richer than the farmers, and had been there longer. They set up the influential Wyoming Stock Growers' Association, to which the state governor belonged. Through this they managed to control the financial policy of the territory and to get laws passed which served their own interests.

The mid-1880s were disastrous years for ranchers all over the Great Plains (see pages 71–72). Homesteaders took over land from bankrupt ranchers. Every time a farmer claimed land, especially if it was around a water hole, and fenced it off, the cattlemen's anger and resentment grew. Gradually the community became divided into two hostile groups. The 'trigger' which set the community ablaze, however, was not the fencing of the land, but cattle rustling.

Cattle rustling

Cattle rustling, or cattle stealing, was always a problem for cattlemen. The Wyoming Stock Growers' Association decided to hire a gang of gun-fighters to track down the rustlers. Their chief was Frank Canton, who had once been sheriff of Johnson County and who was an ex-bank robber and a killer.

Soon the Wyoming Stock Growers' Association had 'proof' of some cattle rustling. Ella Watson and Jim Averill lived together just outside Johnson County. Jim ran a small store, post office and saloon. Ella was a Canadian prostitute who took in visiting cowboys. The problem was that the cowboys often paid Ella with the odd cow or two instead of with money. To complicate matters, Jim and Ella lived on land owned by a rancher called Albert Bothwell. He suspected them of rustling. Matters came to a head over a letter Jim wrote to the *Weekly Mail* in April 1889. In this letter Jim had said that ranchers were nothing but rich land-grabbers. Albert had had enough. In July 1889 he and some friends arrived at Jim and Ella's cabin, and hanged them side by side on a nearby tree. There had been no trial.

Source 1

Contemporary engraving showing Ella Watson and Jim Averill hanging from a tree, Wyoming 1889.

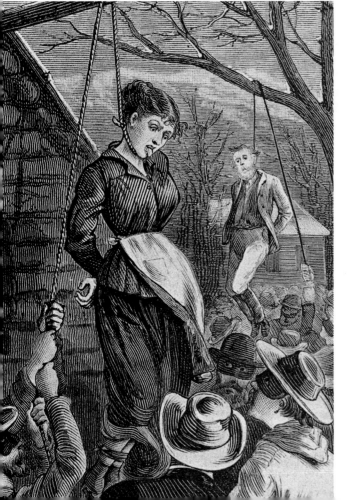

Source 2

Photographs of Jim Averill and Ella Watson, shortly before they were hanged.

Source 3

The Denver News, 1892.

* **ascertained** Discovered or found out.

The cattlemen attack the 'rustlers'

Other killings followed, and the rustling continued. The Wyoming Stock Growers' Association's next move was to draw up a list of about 70 men they thought were involved in rustling. Some of these people may have been rustlers but most were probably innocent settlers. The Association had a list of suspects, but it was determined to find them guilty. They formed a Vigilance Committee, called the 'Regulators'.

The homesteaders decided to arm themselves, and they elected as sheriff 'Red' Angus, who was sympathetic to their cause.

In April 1892 Wyoming was invaded by Frank Canton and the gun-men the Association originally hired to root out the rustlers. The *Denver News* published this account of the battle which followed:

> Forty-six men killed in Wyoming yesterday.
> Nate Champion and fifty men are surrounded by 100 men at the TA Ranch. Two hundred shots have been discharged, but the damage done on either side cannot be ascertained.*
> A number of men are known to have been wounded and some killed. About 100 rustlers have passed through town en route to the scene of the battle to help Champion and his men.

A homesteader had seen Champion's death, and realised that men were on their way to attack the settlers. The homesteader took the news to Buffalo, the nearest town. There the citizens were outraged. Sheriff Angus, getting no help from the military at the nearby Fort McKinney, or from the National Guard, organised a posse to ride out to arrest the invading ranchers. The invaders were now heading for Buffalo. Hearing that the town was up in arms, most of the ranchers decided to make for the TA Ranch and dig themselves in. The TA Ranch was surrounded by angry settlers, led by 'Red' Angus.

The US government intervenes

Word soon got through to the Governor of Wyoming, and even to Benjamin Harrison, the President of the USA. He thought that the whole of Johnson County was in a state of rebellion and ordered troops to be sent to restore the peace. They surrounded the TA Ranch. Three days after the siege had begun the ranchers surrendered to the US forces. The federal troops had promised not to hand over the ranchers to the state

Source 4

The Johnson County War.

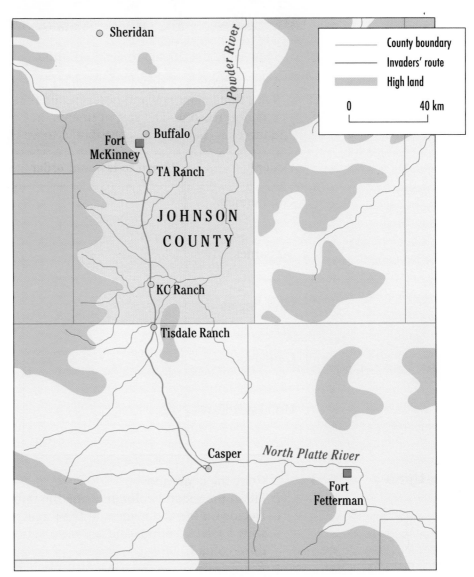

	County boundary
	Invaders' route
	High land

0   40 km

authorities at Buffalo. Instead, the ranchers were handed over to the civil authorities at Cheyenne, where they were well known and amongst friends.

There was no real victory for either side. The invaders were not punished and yet the homesteaders could claim a victory since they stayed where they were. The ranchers began to enclose their ranges. The open range was at an end.

Questions

1   Look at Sources 1 and 2. Use what you know about the situation in Wyoming to explain the difference between them.

2   Explain carefully the different sorts of problems created by:
a fencing the land
b cattle rustling.

3   Who, in your judgement, really won the Johnson County War?

How were the threats to law and order in the West overcome?

Various groups of people threatened law and order in the West. They threatened law and order in different ways and for different reasons. The sort of threats they made were not equally dangerous, but they all contributed to an explosive situation.

Group	Threat to law and order	Seriousness of threat
Gold miners		
Vigilantes		
Gunslingers		
Cattlemen		
Homesteaders		

Questions

1   **a** Copy the chart above.
  b Fill in the second column, using the information in this unit.
  c Decide on the seriousness of the threat, using a scale of 1–5, with 1 = least serious and 5 = most serious. Now fill in the third column.

2   Look back to pages 34–35, which describe how the US government gradually extended the rule of law westwards.

Use this information, the information in the grid and 'The US government intervenes' (pages 94–95) and write a paragraph to describe how the US government brought law and order to the West.

Unit 8 · The struggle for the Great Plains

The US government was determined that white Americans would fulfil their 'manifest destiny' (see Unit 3) and settle the whole of America from the east coast to the west. However, the Great Plains and the whole of the American West were not vast, empty places waiting for white people to take over. They were populated by thousands of Indians. The white people and the Indians wanted the same land. The white people wanted to make the land work for them: to feed cattle, to yield gold and minerals and to grow crops so that they could make a profit and become wealthy. The Indians wanted to work with the land: the land, the Indians and the Great Spirit were one great circle of being. Very, very few white people and Indians understood each other. They feared each other, fought each other and betrayed each other as they struggled for possession of the Great Plains.

Early days: 1825–50

Ever since the days of the first white settlers in the sixteenth century, white people had been buying land from Indians in exchange for money, guns or other goods. However, by the nineteenth century, land-hungry settlers wanted the Indians out of the eastern states. The obvious place to send them, so the white Americans believed, was west of the Mississippi into the Louisiana Purchase, bought from France by President Jefferson in 1803 (see page 5). Here was the Great American Desert, where no white people would ever settle.

The 'Permanent Indian Frontier'

In 1825 the government began moving the Cherokees, Creeks, Chickasaws, Choctaws and Seminoles from the south-east to an area on the eastern fringe of the Great Plains which is now the state of Oklahoma. In 1832 a special US government department was set up to deal with Indian affairs. It quickly decided that the whole of the Great Plains could be given to the Indian tribes. The Great American Desert would be 'One Big Reservation' behind the 95th meridian, which was to be the Permanent Indian Frontier. By 1840 all the eastern Indian tribes had been moved into this new Indian Territory. Source 1 suggests what the forced removal was like for some Indians.

Source 1

Francis Parkman in his book *The Oregon Trail*, 1968.

* **compressed** Pushed together.
* **plundered** Robbed.

They were ill-looking fellows, thin and swarthy, with care-worn, anxious faces, and lips rigidly compressed*. Since leaving the settlements they had met with nothing but misfortune. Some of their party had died; one man had been killed by the Pawnees; and about a week before they had been plundered* by the Dahcotahs (Sioux) of all their best horses.

Settlers move west: the Indian policy changes

Policy of concentration

The Mountain Indians

White people who crossed the Great Plains began to demand protection from Indian attacks. The US government came up with the same solution. The northern mountain Indians, like the Snakes, Bannocks and Ute, did not hunt or live off the buffalo, and did not put up much resistance to the government's proposals. By 1868 they had agreed to move to special areas. However, the south-western Indians, such as the warlike Apache and Navaho, were a different matter. They resisted fiercely any attempt to drive them off their lands, but in the end even they had to give in to the US army. The Navahos finally agreed to live in an area near Fort Sumner on the Pecos River (see the map on page 63) where most of them became farmers. Between 1871 and 1874 the US army moved the Apaches to New Mexico and Arizona.

The Plains Indians

The Plains Indians presented the US government with a tremendous problem. They needed to roam the Great Plains, following the great herds of buffalo. On the other hand, white people needed to be able to cross the Plains without fear of attack. Some of the Plains Indians, like the Arapahos and the Kiowas, had shown friendliness to the white people, and were less warlike than others. It was only because there was an increasing number of white people taking the trails west in the 1840s and 1850s that the Plains Indians felt threatened and began to attack wagon trains and mail coaches.

In 1849 the US government made treaties with the Comanches and the Kiowas. The Indians agreed to allow US citizens to cross their lands and to stop attacking white travellers on the Santa Fe Trail. This was to be the new government policy. Indians and white people signed treaties whereby the Indians promised not to attack travellers in return for protection and guaranteed land.

The Fort Laramie Treaty, 1851

The Cheyenne and Arapaho lived in the central Plains around the North and South Platte Rivers and the Arkansas River. As more and more travellers took to the Oregon Trail, the Indians became restless and began attacking the wagon trains. In 1851 Thomas Fitzpatrick, the government Indian agent controlling the Platte River outpost, called together the chiefs of the main Plains tribes for a meeting near Fort Laramie (see the map on page 63). His job was to get the Indians to sign the sort of treaty agreed two years earlier between the US government and the Comanches and Kiowa. He succeeded. The Indians agreed to the terms of the Fort Laramie Treaty which gave them lands – they believed forever – along

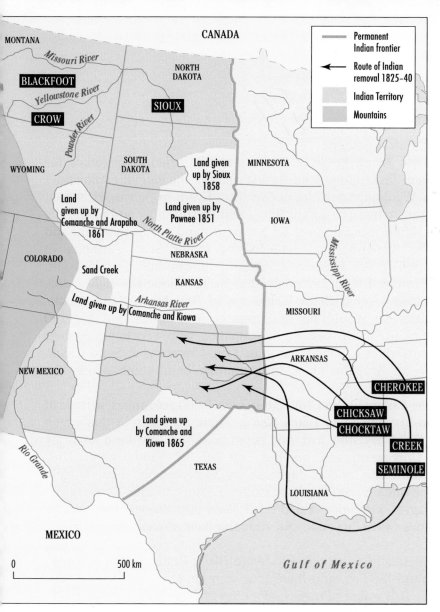

Source 1

Land of the Plains Indians in 1865.

the foothills of the Rocky Mountains between the North Platte and Arkansas Rivers. The government promised to protect them, and pay the tribes $50,000 a year for ten years. In return, the Indians agreed to stop attacking travellers on the Oregon Trail, and to allow the government to build roads and military posts.

This policy became known as 'concentration' because the Indians were put together in certain areas. The days of the 'One Big Reservation' were over. So were the days of the Permanent Indian Frontier.

The Fort Lyon Treaty, 1861

In 1859 gold was discovered at Pike's Peak in the Colorado Mountains (see pages 54–55). White men surged through the Cheyenne and Arapaho lands, forgetting (if, indeed, they had ever known) the agreements made with the Indians. Miners and other settlers moved on to Indian lands in Kansas and Nebraska. The railroad companies demanded the removal of Indians and buffalo from the routes along which they planned to build railroads across the Great Plains. Then, in 1861, Colorado became a territory. It now officially belonged to white Americans.

The Indians, however, remembered the white American's promises, and soon took their revenge. Both Arapahos and Cheyennes began serious attacks on railroad surveyors and travellers. In 1861 the government called the tribal chiefs to a conference at Fort Lyon. There they forced the chiefs to agree to abandon claims to land given them under the Fort Laramie Treaty. Instead, the government gave them a small reservation between the Arkansas River and Sand Creek in eastern Colorado.

Indian chiefs, however, had no power to force their people to do anything. Most warriors refused to accept the Fort Lyon Treaty. They went on the warpath, raiding mining camps and attacking mail coaches in Colorado and New Mexico. The carefully worked out treaties clearly had not worked for the US government.

Questions

1 **a** What was the 'Permanent Indian Frontier'?
  b Why did the US government introduce it?

2 Why did both Indians and the US government break the Fort Laramie and Fort Lyon Treaties?

The Plains wars

The Sand Creek massacre

In August 1864 Black Kettle, a Cheyenne chief, tried to negotiate for peace. He went first to Major Edward Wynkoop, the federal commander at Fort Lyon. Wynkoop took him to Governor Evans in Denver. However, Governor Evans refused to accept Black Kettle's surrender and to end the wars. Black Kettle could do nothing but return and set up camp at Sand Creek. When Wynkoop was replaced by Major Scott Anthony in November 1864, Black Kettle tried again. Anthony first promised him army protection and then, uncertain that he had done the right thing, withdrew it and ordered Black Kettle out of Fort Lyon. Black Kettle, apparently sure he would be protected by US troops, led his 700 Cheyenne back to Sand Creek. Some Arapahos, who were camping near Fort Lyon, moved away. One band joined the Cheyenne at Sand Creek. Little Raven, an Arapaho chief, took another band south across the Arkansas River.

Meanwhile, Colonel John Chivington, with 1,000 volunteers, arrived at Fort Lyon in hot pursuit of Black Kettle. There he was told that Black Kettle and the Cheyenne had not been promised any kind of army protection. Chivington and his men set off for Sand Creek. They surrounded the camp, and at daybreak on 29 November they charged. They took the Indians completely by surprise. Though Black Kettle raised the white flag of surrender and the US Stars and Stripes, the soldiers slaughtered over 450 Cheyenne and Arapaho men, women and children.

Source 1

An account of the Sand Creek massacre by Robert Bent, the half-Cheyenne son of rancher William Bent. Robert Bent was forced by Chivington to go as a guide in search of Black Kettle's camp. This account was given as evidence to the US Senate Committee of Enquiry.

I saw the American flag waving and heard Black Kettle tell the Indians to stand around the flag, and there they were huddled – men, women and children. This was when we were within fifty yards of the Indians. I also saw a white flag raised. These flags were in so conspicuous a place that they must have been seen. I think there were 600 Indians in all. I think there were thirty-five braves and some old men, about sixty in all. The rest of the men were away from camp, hunting. I saw five squaws under a bank for shelter. When the troops came up to them they ran off and begged for mercy, but the soldiers shot them all. There were some thirty or forty squaws collected in a hole for protection. They sent out a little girl about six years old with a white flag on a stick. She had not proceeded more than a few steps when she was shot and killed. All the squaws in the hole were killed. Every one I saw dead was scalped. I saw quite a number of infants in arms killed with their mothers.

Source 2

Part of the evidence given by Lieutenant James Connor to the US Senate Committee of Enquiry.

In going over the battleground next day I did not see a body of man, woman or child but was scalped, and in many instances their bodies were mutilated in the most horrible manner – men and women's privates cut out, etc. – According to my best knowledge and belief these atrocities that were committed were with the knowledge of J. M. Chivington, and I do not know of his taking any measures to prevent them.

Source 3

Part of the evidence given by Stephen Decatur, Colorado cavalryman, to the US Senate Committee of Enquiry.

The next day after the battle I went over the battleground and counted 450 dead Indian warriors. I took pleasure in going as, the evening before, while the village was being burned, I saw something which made me feel as though I should have liked to have spent a little more time fighting. I saw some of the men opening bundles and taking from them a number of white person's scalps. I saw one scalp of a white woman in particular. The hair was auburn and hung in ringlets. It was very long hair.

Source 4

Part of the evidence given by Lieutenant Cramer to the US Senate Committee of Enquiry.

It was a mistake that there was any white scalps found in the village. I saw one but it was very old, the hair being much faded. We arrived at the village about daylight. The women and children were huddled together, and most of our fire concentrated on them. The Indian warriors, about 100 in number, fought desperately. I told Colonel Chivington it would be murder if he attacked those Indians. His reply was, bringing his fist close to my face, 'Damn any man who sympathises with Indians.' He had come to kill Indians and believed it would be honourable to kill any Indians under any and all circumstances.

Source 5

Colonel Chivington, in a public speech made in Denver, shortly before the Sand Creek massacre.

Kill and scalp all, big and little. Nits make lice.

Black Kettle managed to escape from Sand Creek, and carried news of the massacre to other tribes. Immediately the Cheyennes, Arapahos, Comanches and Kiowas increased their attacks on ranches, mail coaches and travellers. Any troops sent against them were resisted with bloody violence.

What Colonel Chivington had done horrified both white men and Indians. Both now demanded an end to the wars. The government set up a Committee of Enquiry (see Sources 1–4) which, having considered all the evidence, declared: 'He deliberately planned and executed a foul and dastardly massacre which would have disgraced the most savage among those who were the victims of his cruelty.'

The meeting at Bluff Creek, October 1865

The US government peace commission and the Indian chiefs met at Bluff Creek, on the Arkansas River. Black Kettle, for the Cheyenne and Little Raven for the Arapaho agreed to lay down their arms and give up Sand Creek in return for money and land in Oklahoma. The Kiowas and the Comanches agreed to go to a reservation in north-west Texas, and to give up all claims to central and western Texas, and eastern New Mexico. There was, for a time, peace in the south-western Plains. This was not, however, the end of the Plains wars. The Sioux were still resisting the US government in the northern Plains, and this could break the fragile peace in the south-western Plains.

After the Civil War

In April 1865 the Civil War ended. The US government succeeded in uniting the north and south into one Union. It was now time to unite the east and west of America. In charge of doing this was General William

Photograph of General William Tecumseh Sherman. His second name was that of a famous Shawnee Indian chief.

Tecumseh Sherman. He had a tremendous task. He had to deal with hostile Indians and settlers demanding protection; with newspapers in the east that were always ready to blame the army for any harm that came to the Indians; with newspapers in the west that were urging the army to deal harshly with the Indians, and with a government that never seemed sure whether it wanted to make peace with the Indians or wipe them out. Sherman made his own attitude to the Indians quite clear:

> The nomad Indians should be removed from the vicinity of [the land around] the two great railroads, and localised on one of the two reservations south of Kansas and north of Nebraska. This would leave for our people exclusively the use of the wide belt of land between the Platte and Arkansas rivers.

Source 7 General Sherman, quoted in *The Wild West*, Channel 4.

In August 1865, while Sherman was getting to grips with the work he had to do, John Pope, one of his officers, began a military campaign against the Plains Indians. He moved the soldiers under his command on to the plains of Kansas and up the Missouri River into Dakota. Three more troops of soldiers marched into Wyoming.

The Bozeman Trail

The discovery of gold in Montana (see page 55) did not only give the government problems as far as law and order were concerned. It also gave them problems with the Indians. The fastest route to the gold fields of Montana was along the Bozeman Trail. This ran through the Cheyenne, Arapaho and Sioux hunting country in the foothills of the Big Horns, where the water and grass were sweet and there were plenty of buffalo, bear, deer, antelope and elk. There were few problems when the Bozeman Trail was little used, but now thousands of white men began to stream along it with their wagons and handcarts, and hopes of a fortune. The Indians, led by a Lakota chief, Red Cloud, took to the warpath.

Source 8

Red Cloud, quoted in *The Wild West*, Channel 4.

> The white men have crowded the Indians back year by year until we are forced to live in a small country north of the Platte, and now our last hunting ground, the home of the People, is to be taken from us. Our women and children will starve, but for my part, I prefer to die fighting.

John Pope was determined to defeat the Indians and keep the Bozeman Trail open. He ordered the building of a fort on the Powder River and sent a fighting force of well-equipped soldiers deep into Lakota territory. Their orders were to kill every Indian they found who was over 12 years old. The Lakota-Sioux and Cheyenne, however, had other ideas. War parties kept attacking the soldiers all through the summer, and by the autumn hundreds of soldiers had deserted.

The government then turned to its well-tried technique of offering the

Indians protection and money in return for peace. At the last moment, Red Cloud discovered that the army was planning to build at least two more forts along the Bozeman Trail. He stormed out of the meeting. The Indians kept up the pressure, attacking soldiers who were building the forts. By December 1866 the situation was at breaking point.

Source 9

The Bozeman Trail.

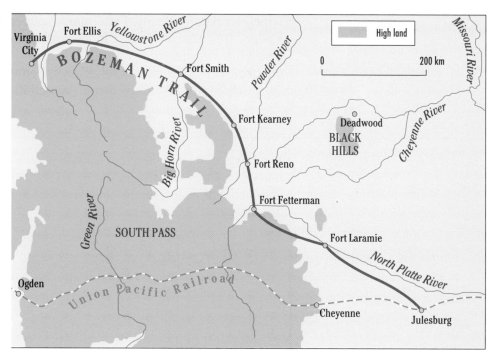

Source 10

An eye-witness describes what he felt when he saw the results of an attack by Indians on a US army division. In W. A. Bell, *New Tracks in North America Vol. 1*, 1869.

I have seen in days gone by sights horrible and gory, but never did I feel the sickening sensation, the giddy, fainting feeling that came over me when I saw our dead, dying and wounded after this Indian fight. The bugler was stripped naked, and five arrows driven through him while his skull was literally smashed to atoms. Another soldier was shot with four bullets and three arrows, his scalp was torn off and his brains knocked out. Sergeant Wylyams lay dead beside the mangled horse. The muscles of the right arms, hacked to the bone, speak of the Cheyenne. The nose slit denotes the Arapaho. The cut throat bears witness that the Sioux were also present.

Fetterman's trap

On 21 December 1866 a wagon train bringing wood to the forts sent a message to Fort Kearney asking for help. They were under constant attack from Indians, and couldn't hold out for much longer. Colonel Henry Carrington, who was in charge of the Montana district, agreed that Captain William J. Fetterman could take some soldiers and deal with the situation. Carrington made his position clear in the order he gave to Fetterman:

Source 11

Colonel Henry Carrington's orders to Captain Fetterman, 1866.

Support the wood-train. Relieve it and report to me. Do not engage or pursue Indians at its expense. Under no circumstances pursue over the ridge, that is, Lodge Trail Ridge.

Carrington and his 80 men left Fort Kearney, aiming to teach the Indians a lesson they would not forget. Every time the soldiers got to within firing distance of the Indians, Crazy Horse and his fellow braves fell back, always just out of reach of Fetterman and his men. The Indians taunted the soldiers, drawing them further and further away from the safety of the fort. Gradually Crazy Horse and his men drew the troops into a trap, which worked perfectly. Fetterman's soldiers followed Crazy Horse over Lodge Trail Ridge. Red Cloud, and hundreds of Lakota-Sioux and Cheyenne braves, were waiting for them on the other side. The Indians attacked. No US soldier was left alive. Fetterman and another officer shot each other in order to avoid capture and disgrace.

Questions

1 Read Sources 1-4, which are all eye-witness accounts of the Sand Creek massacre. Copy out the grid below. For each source, list what is said about the things on the left of the grid. Then answer all parts of question 2.

	Source 1	Source 2	Source 3	Source 4
flags number of warriors/braves killing of women scalping of Indians mutilations of Indians dead Indians white scalps				

2 **a** Which sources give similar information on these points? In what ways?
b Which sources give different information on these points? In what ways?
c Which of these accounts contradict each other on these points? In what ways?
d What reasons can you think of for any differences or contradictions?

3 During the American Civil War, Southern Confederate soldiers and Northern 'Yankee' soldiers did not scalp each other during a battle. Use any of the sources and the information in this section which might help to explain why they scalped Indians.

4 Who was to blame for Fetterman's trap? (Think about long-term and short-term causes.)

A new policy: small reservations

By 1867 many people were beginning to believe that a new policy toward the Indians was needed. More and more white Americans were beginning to realise that much of the trouble was caused by white people moving over and settling on land that had been given to the Indians in various treaties. These treaties had been broken by both whites and Indians. The basic problem was that the Great Plains were no longer, as the US government had thought in the 1840s, useless to anyone but the Indians. White people wanted them: but so did the Indians.

In March 1867 the US government set up a peace commission to try and solve the Indian problem once and for all. The members of the commission agreed that the peace treaties made with the Indians had not worked. The policy of 'concentration' should end. Instead, the Indian tribes should be put separately in small reservations. White Americans would teach them to become farmers and to live as white people did, but out of the way of settlers, miners and soldiers. The areas which the commission thought would be ideal for this were the Indian Territory of Oklahoma, and the Black Hills of Dakota.

The Medicine Lodge Creek meeting, 1867
The commissioners met representatives of the southern Plains tribes at Medicine Lodge Creek in October 1867. The Kiowas and Comanches had been peaceful since they had been moved from their old hunting grounds in 1865. They did not see why they should move again. However, they were bribed and threatened until they agreed to move to a reservation of 3 million acres between the Red and the Washita Rivers, in Indian Territory. The Cheyennes and the Arapahos accepted a sandy and barren area between the Cimmaron and Arkansas Rivers, also in Indian Territory.

The Fort Laramie Treaty, 1868
The commissioners held a separate meeting with the chiefs of the northern tribes. One of their aims was also to end the Plains wars in which the southern tribes were not involved. The government realised that the main problem was the Bozeman Trail, and by the time the commissioners had reached Fort Laramie in the spring of 1868, they had decided to give way to the Indians and abandon the Trail. Red Cloud agreed to what the commissioners proposed. The government said it would stop work on the Bozeman Trail (officially called the Powder River Road) and would abandon three forts. In return for this, Red Cloud, a Lakota-Sioux chief, agreed to take his people to a permanent reservation in Dakota, stretching from the Black Hills to the Missouri. Additionally, they could use their old hunting grounds in the Big Horn country as long as the government did not want them. Red Cloud was pleased with this latest agreement. When the soldiers left the forts, he and his warriors burned them down. He believed he had won the Plains wars.

Source 1

Part of the Fort Laramie Treaty between the US government and Red Cloud, 1868.

From this day forward all war between the parties to this agreement shall forever cease. The government of the United States desires peace, and its honour is hereby pledged to keep it. The Indians desire peace, and they now pledge their honour to maintain it.

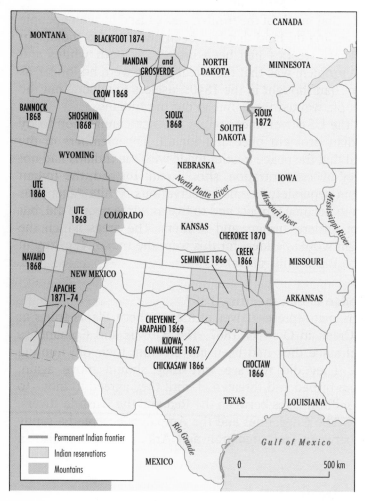

Permanent Indian frontier
Indian reservations
Mountains

Source 2

Indian reservations in 1875.

Small reservations: the answer?

In the summer and autumn of 1868 the government extended its 'small reservation' policy to the Rocky Mountain area. The tribes there, such as the Ute, the Arapaho, the Shoshoni and the Apache, agreed to go to small reservations scattered throughout Colorado, Idaho, Wyoming, Arizona and New Mexico.

At first it seemed that Indians and white people would be able to live in peace. However, each side had problems which were to make this impossible. Indians in reservations could not lead their old, nomadic way of life. They had to depend, not on meat that they had themselves hunted and killed, but on food brought in from outside. Many of them were miserable, and longed for a life on the open plains. Many young warriors refused to accept the agreements made by their chiefs, and were ready to fight for the old way of life. The white people, for their part, were not to know that they would soon want the Black Hills of Dakota.

Questions

1 **a** Why did the US government decide to introduce a new Indian policy in 1867?
   b What was 'new' about this policy?

2 These are the words of Red Cloud:

Quoted in Dee Brown, *Bury my Heart at Wounded Knee*, 1971.

Whose voice was first sounded on this land? The voice of the red people who had bows and arrows. What has been done in my country I did not want, did not ask for it; when the white man comes in my country he leaves a trail of blood behind him. I have two mountains in that country – the Black Hills and the Big Horn mountain. I want the Great Father (the USA President) to make no roads through them.

What arguments would US government officials use against what Red Cloud was saying?

Conflict again: Sheridan, Sherman and Custer

The Indian peace policy

President Ulysses S. Grant, who became US President in 1869, developed an Indian peace policy. He wanted to make sure that the Indian agents, the white men who were in charge of Indian affairs, were the right sort of men. He believed it was important that the Indians were treated with care and respect. He also tried to see that the right sort of supplies reached the Indians on the reservations, and that the supplies were in good condition.

However, the efforts of those put in charge of the US government's Indian policy by President Grant could not solve the basic problem. The whole idea behind the reservations was that the Indians should learn the white way of life. They were to learn how to plough and sow and reap. They were to attend school and learn to read, write and do simple sums:

Source 1

Big Eagle, a Sioux chief. Quoted in Dee Brown, *Bury my Heart at Wounded Knee*, 1971.

The whites were always trying to make the Indians give up their life and live like white men – go to farming, work hard and do as they did – and the Indians did not know how to do that, and did not want it anyway.

If the Indians were to live like white people, they would have to accept a totally different view of the land, and this was more than many of them could do:

Source 2

Chief Joseph, of the Nez Perce, quoted in Dee Brown, *Bury my Heat at Wounded Knee*, 1971.

The earth was created by the assistance of the sun, and should be left as it is. The earth and myself are of one mind. The measure of the land and the measure of our bodies are the same. I never said the land was mine to do with as I chose. The one who has the right to dispose of it is the one who has created it.

The white person's view of the land was quite different:

Source 3

The Authorized Version of the Bible, Genesis 1:28.

* **replenish** Put back what has been taken, refresh.
* **subdue** To bring under control, to farm.

God said unto them, Be fruitful, and multiply, and replenish* the earth, and subdue* it; and have dominion over the fish of the sea, and over the fowl of the air, and over every living thing that moveth upon the earth.

The Battle of the River Washita

It was the army which really decided the fate of the Indians. In the autumn of 1868 Generals Sherman and Sheridan asked for, and got, the services of General George Armstrong Custer. He had fought with them in the Civil War, and they knew that, with his skill and daring, they would be able to subdue the Indians forever. They also knew that he was hot-headed, self-confident, prone to disobey orders – and was just coming to the end of a year's suspension from his regiment.

General Sheridan, who was in charge of the army in the West, decided to plan a winter campaign. Indians did not, as a rule, roam the Great

Source 4

General Philip H. Sheridan.

Plains in winter. He believed it would be an easy job to hunt down the Indians when they were in their winter camps. The plan was to have two columns of troops to drive the Indians into the Washita River valley in Indian Territory (Oklahoma). Here the main force, commanded by General George A. Custer, would be waiting to crush the Indians. However, things didn't quite turn out as planned.

Custer marched south, with his men, into Indian Territory to take up position in the Washita valley. Unexpectedly, his scouts picked up the trail of some Indians. Forgetting orders, Custer ordered his men in pursuit. Four days later, at midnight on 27 November, they reached the Indian camp. Custer had no idea whose camp it was, nor whether the Indians were hostile or friendly. At dawn Custer and his men attacked. The Indians fled, screaming, and were cut down by the soldiers. Soon it was all over. Black Kettle, the Cheyenne peace chief, and his wife were shot in the back as they tried to escape through the icy waters of the River Washita. Altogether Custer and his men killed 103 Indians: 11 warriors and 92 women, children and old men.

Throughout the winter of 1868–9, the army attacked Indians on the central and southern Plains. Bands of weary, defeated Indians straggled in to Fort Cobb, on the River Washita, to surrender. The army sent the Kiowa and Comanche to those lands which had been assigned to them in the Medicine Lodge Treaty. They sent the Cheyenne and the Arapaho to a reservation along the upper Washita River.

Source 5

'Attack at dawn'. A painting by C. Schreyvogel of Custer's attack on Black Kettle in his Washita River valley camp.

Source 6

Dee Brown's account of the mustering of the Indians at Fort Cobb in 1868. Quoted in *Bury my Heart at Wounded Knee*, 1971.

Yellow Bear of the Arapahos also agreed to bring his people to Fort Cobb. A few days later, Tosawi brought in the first band of Comanches to surrender. When he was presented to Sheridan, Tosawi's eyes brightened. He spoke his own name and added two words of broken English 'Tosawi, good Indian', he said. It was then that General Sheridan uttered the immortal words 'The only good Indians I ever saw were dead.'

Question

1   **a** What was President Grant's Indian peace policy?
     b Why did this policy fail?

The Battle of Little Big Horn

The final, decisive battle between the whites and Indians was to begin in the Black Hills of Dakota: a sacred place for the Cheyenne, Arapaho and Sioux Indians, and a place rich in gold.

Source 1

Stephen E. Ambrose, *Crazy Horse and Custer: the parallel lives of two American warriors*, 1975.

The white man writing the treaties never meant a word that he said. When we wrote a treaty that said 'You will have the Black Hills as long as the grass shall grow', we never meant that. It was outright lies. The treaties didn't hold because one party to them never meant them to hold. It was criminal, in my view, to lie to the Indians in the way we did.

Source 2

General George Armstrong Custer.

Events leading to the battle

Gold in the Black Hills

For many years there had been rumours of gold in the Black Hills of Dakota. However, by the terms of the Fort Laramie Treaty of 1868, whites were forbidden to prospect there, and the Indians were not interested in gold. However, the Northern Pacific Railroad was fast approaching Sioux hunting grounds in Dakota. General George Custer was put in charge of the soldiers sent to protect the railroad surveyors from Indian attacks. The Indians were angry that the railroad was being built. They were also angry that this railroad brought hundreds of white buffalo hunters on to the Plains who killed buffalo for their skins and wasted the meat. At the same time, the economic depression of 1873 meant that there was tremendous pressure on the authorities to allow white men to prospect for gold in the Black Hills.

Custer was not only in Dakota to protect railroad surveyors. He was there to find gold. On 2 July 1874 he led an expedition from Fort Abraham Lincoln into the Black Hills. Twenty-five days later they struck gold, and within six months thousands of white prospectors poured into the Black Hills, staking claims to land the Sioux believed to be theirs by right and by US law. The US government then tried to buy back the Black Hills from the Indians. They offered $6 million, but Red Cloud held out for more, plus cash and rations for seven generations to come, and the talks broke down. The government lost patience. President Grant ordered all Indians into reservations within 60 days. After that date, any still outside would be considered hostile and could be attacked by any soldiers who came across them. Sitting Bull of the Hunkpapa-Sioux and Crazy Horse of the Lakota-Sioux, refused and prepared for war.

Rosebud River

All through the spring of 1876 scattered bands of Sioux, Arapaho and Cheyenne joined Sitting Bull and Crazy Horse. By the end of May, more than 7,000 Indians, 2,000 of whom were warriors, had erected around 1000 lodges on lands between the Powder River and Rosebud River. On 4 June Sitting Bull moved his Indians to the valley of Rosebud River and ordered the Sun Dance (see page 13) to begin. After four days Sitting Bull had a tremendous vision. He saw white men falling head first into the Sioux camp and he heard a voice telling him that the white men had no ears. The Indians believed this meant that they would defeat the white men, who had not listened to the Indians' requests for peace.

General George Crook had been looking for the camps of the Sioux, Arapaho and Cheyenne and had not found them. The Indians, however, found the soldiers. Mid-morning on 17 June, Crazy Horse and 1,500 Lakota and Cheyenne warriors, inspired by the Sun Dance, swept down on the army camp. By nightfall 84 soldiers were dead and Crook and his defeated men had retreated south to their base camp on Goose Creek.

Source 3

Private Phineas Towne, who was part of General Crook's troop of soldiers. Quoted in *The Wild West*, Channel 4.

You can talk of seeing devils; there they were in full form, painted in the most terrifying manner, some with war bonnets adorned with horns of steers and buffalo. It was enough to strike terror to anyone's heart.

This was not, however, to be the final conflict of Sitting Bull's vision. After Rosebud River, Sitting Bull and Crazy Horse led their people west, towards the river the Indians had named Greasy Grass River, and which the whites called the Little Big Horn.

Custer's Last Stand

General Alfred Terry, who was responsible for this particular campaign against the Indians, did not want Sitting Bull and Crazy Horse to slip away. He thought he knew where they were and, after General Crook's defeat, wanted to end the Indian menace once and for all. He ordered Colonel John Gibbon to take a column of infantry eastwards out of Fort Ellis along the valley of the Yellowstone River to where it met the Big Horn River. They were to attack the Indian camp from the north. Meanwhile, General Custer, with the much faster 7th Cavalry, was to find and follow the Indians' trail before it went cold, locate their camp precisely, and attack from the south in a combined assault with the infantry.

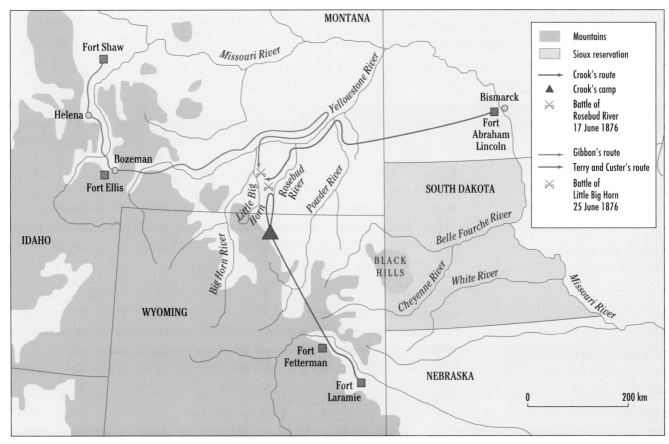

Source 4

Map of the Big Horn area.

The 7th cavalry made good speed, and quickly picked up the Indian trail. Within two days they reached the place where Sitting Bull had held his Sun Dance before the Battle of Rosebud River; a short time later they found a wide area of flattened grass where thousands of Indians had crossed the Rosebud River, heading west. On 25 June 1876, Custer and his men were within 15 miles of the Little Big Horn. At dawn, Custer's Indian scouts spotted the Indian camp. It was the biggest camp ever seen on the Great Plains. Custer's scouts warned him that the 7th Cavalry didn't have enough bullets to kill all the Indians they had seen. That didn't seem to bother Custer:

Source 5

General George Custer: June 1876. Quoted in *The Wild West*, Channel 4.

The largest Indian camp on the North American continent is ahead and I am going to attack it.

Custer decided to attack at once. He split his men into three groups. Captain Frederick Benteen took three companies and moved west. Major Marcus Reno took another three companies and prepared to attack the camp from the south. Custer himself went along the north bank of the Rosebud River with the remaining five companies of soldiers. The attack went badly wrong from the start. Reno's charge was quickly stopped by hordes of Lakota warriors. The remnants of his division were met by Benteen, who realised Reno needed help badly. He regrouped Reno's men and did his best to fortify the hilltop they were occupying. They managed to hold the hilltop, but were kept there by hundreds of Indians. Custer and his men were left alone and without support. They were engaged in a fight to the death. No one knows what really happened. Archaeological evidence seems to suggest that Custer and his men never managed to cross the Little Big Horn River. As they approached a shallow ford, they were met by 1,500 Indian warriors on horseback. They retreated, fighting all the way and trying desperately to reach higher ground. Just as they reached the top of a rise, and comparative safety, Crazy Horse and 1,000 Oglala Sioux and Cheyenne warriors came pouring over, sweeping away everything in front of them and firing from the very latest repeating rifles. Some of Custer's men may have fought bravely to the end; some may have fled in panic; others may have shot themselves to avoid mutilation by the Indians. Whatever happened, it probably lasted for about an hour.

Late on 26 June the Indians began to withdraw. They took down their tipis, set fire to the prairie and headed for the Big Horn mountains. Sitting Bull's vision had come true: they had won.

When General Terry arrived on 27 June with the main army he found the dead bodies of all 225 of Custer's men. Most of them had been stripped, disfigured and scalped. Custer's brother, Tom, was so badly mutilated that he could only be identified by a tattoo on his arm. General Custer had been shot twice: through the left temple and the heart. Apart from that, his body seemed to have been untouched. He had not been scalped and he had not been stripped. Eight days later the whole of America heard of the massacre.

Source 6

A reconstruction of the Battle of Little Big Horn, painted by Edgar Paxson in 1899 after a good deal of research. Custer is in the picture, top centre.

Source 7

The Battle of Little Big Horn, painted by Kicking Bear. This is the only painting by an eyewitness known to exist. Custer is lying left of centre, and standing in the centre are the chiefs Sitting Bull, Rain-in-the-Face, Crazy Horse and Kicking Bear.

What really happened at Little Big Horn?

One of the problems in trying to find out about what happened at Little Big Horn on 25 June 1876 is that no white man survived, and the Indians that were there have said very little about it. What happened has to be reconstructed from archaeological evidence (this is how we know the Indians used fast repeating rifles) and the Indian evidence that survives (which can be difficult to interpret). Sometimes it is contradictory.

Source 8

Chief Sitting Bull. Reported in *The Wild West*, Channel 4.

They tell me I murdered Custer. It is a lie. He was a fool and rode to his death.

Source 9

B. W. Beacroft, *The Last Fighting Indians of the American West*, 1976.

* **pictograph** Word picture.

Long after the battle, White Bull of the Miniconjous drew four pictographs* showing himself grappling with and killing a soldier identified as Custer. Among others who claimed to have killed Custer were Rain-in-the-Face, Flat Hip and Brave Bear. Red Horse said that an unidentified Santee warrior killed Custer. Most Indians who told of the battle said they never saw Custer and did not know who killed him. 'We did not know till the fight was over that he was the white chief', Low Dog said.

Source 10

Quoted in Dee Brown, *Bury my Heart at Wounded Knee*, 1971.

In an interview given in Canada a year after the battle, Sitting Bull said that he never saw Custer, but that other Indians had seen and recognised him just before he was killed. 'He did not wear his hair long as he used to wear it,' Sitting Bull said, 'It was short.' But Sitting Bull did not say who killed Custer. An Arapaho warrior who was riding with the Cheyenne said that Custer was killed by several Indians. 'He was dressed in buckskin, coat and pants, and was on his hands and knees, he had been shot through the side, and there was blood coming from his mouth. Then the Indians closed in around him, and I did not see any more.'

There seems to have been considerable confusion as to which Indian did actually kill Custer, and there may well be many reasons for this. What is certain is that Custer's body was not mutilated in the ways in which the bodies of other soldiers were damaged. Here again, there are different theories as to why this was:

Source 11

From the introduction written by Kenneth Fenwick, to Custer's book *My Life on the Plains*.

Custer made many friends among the Indians, who trusted him more than they did most white men; and at the end they showed their regard for him by treating his body with unparalleled respect when it lay on his last field.

Kate Bighead, a northern Cheyenne woman, gave a different reason for Custer's body remaining unmutilated:

Source 12

Evans S. Connell, *Son of the Morning Star*, 1985.

Me-ot-zi [a Cheyenne woman]...sometimes went riding with General Custer....Later, after he went away, Me-ot-zi said General Custer was her husband. She said he promised to come back to her....Two southern Cheyenne women were at the Little Big Horn, and when the fighting ended they went to the battlefield. They saw Custer. They knew him well. They recognised him even though his hair was short and his face was dirty. While they stood looking down at him a bunch of Sioux warriors came by and wanted to cut up his body, but the women made signs telling warriors he was a relative.

Questions

1   a What do Indian sources tell us about what happened to General Custer?
    b On what points do the Indian sources agree?
    c On what points do the Indian sources disagree?

2   Sources 6 and 7 both show what happened at Little Big Horn. Which do you think is the more accurate? Why?

Was the Battle of Little Big Horn an Indian victory?

There is no doubt that the Indians defeated Custer and the 7th Cavalry at the Battle of Little Big Horn. It was, however, no real victory for the Indians. In many ways, it hastened their end. The news of the defeat of General Custer spread quickly. White Americans were stunned and horrified. There was enormous pressure on the government to crush the Plains Indians once and for all.

After the battle, the Cheyenne and Sioux bands went their separate ways. However, they did not get very far. Army divisions, led by General Crook and General Terry, pursued them until they finally gave in. By the autumn of 1876 most had drifted back to their reservations, and in the spring of 1877 even Crazy Horse had given in. He was captured by the US army and, in September 1877, killed whilst trying to escape from Fort Robinson. Sitting Bull took his people to Canada, where they hoped for British protection. Shortage of food, however, forced them to return to the United States where they surrendered to government forces in 1881. The heart seemed to have gone out of the Sioux and the Cheyenne. True, they had won at Little Big Horn, but they had lost the Black Hills, their holy place, for good.

The Ghost Dance

Sitting Bull had not completely given up hope. He was determined to protect and keep what land his people still had in the Great Sioux Reservation. He would do this, not by fighting, but by peaceful discussion. The US government, on the other hand, was just as determined to take more Sioux land to satisfy the demands of the homesteaders and settlers who were pouring in from Europe.

In October 1890 Kicking Bear, a Miniconjou Indian, came to Sitting Bull with a strange story. A Paiute medicine man, Wokova, had had a vision:

Source 1

Quoted in Dee Brown, *Bury my heart at Wounded Knee*, 1971.

* **game** Animals.

All Indians must dance, everywhere, keep on dancing. Pretty soon in next spring, Great Spirit come. He bring back all animals of every kind. The game* be thick everywhere. All dead Indians come back and live again. When Great Spirit comes this way, then all the Indians go to the mountains, high away from the whites. Whites can't hurt Indians then. Then while Indians way up high, big flood come like water and all white people die, get drowned. After that, water go way and then nobody but Indians everywhere and game all kinds thick.

Sitting Bull was doubtful about this. He did not mind his people learning the Ghost Dance, but he was afraid the US army might be sent into the reservations to stop the dancing and there would be further conflict. Kicking Bear told him that if they wore special shirts, painted with magic symbols, the soldiers' bullets would not be able to harm them.

The Ghost Dance spread like a prairie fire, and soon it was being danced in every Sioux reservation. White Indian Agents, who managed the reservations, began to get seriously worried. They grew even more worried when some of the dancers began holding rifles over their heads as they danced. US President Harrison ordered the army to take over control of the Indians. When the army commanders discovered that Sitting Bull was one of the chiefs who was encouraging the Ghost Dance, they sent the Reservation Police to arrest him. Early on 15 December 43 police surrounded Sitting Bull's log cabin. They were immediately confronted by large numbers of dancers, shouting 'You shall not take our chief!' In the confusion that followed, shots were fired. Sitting Bull, some other Indians and half a dozen policemen, were killed. The police were buried with full military honours. Sitting Bull's body was buried without any ceremony in a pauper's grave.

The Battle of Wounded Knee

Many of Sitting Bull's followers fled south, believing they would be safer with Big Foot's band of Ghost Dancers in the Cheyenne River Reservation. Big Foot, however, had led the Ghost Dance amongst the Miniconjou Sioux, and orders had gone out for his arrest. On 23 December, in deep snow, Big Foot and his band of 120 men and 230 women and children headed south for the Pine Ridge Reservation. There they hoped that the last great Lakota-Sioux chief, Red Cloud, would give them protection.

The army immediately sent three regiments in hot pursuit. After five days, part of the 7th Cavalry found them. By this time Big Foot was suffering badly from pneumonia, and the rest of the band were in a bad way. The soldiers took them, under armed guard, to Wounded Knee Creek. The following day, 29 December 1890, the cavalrymen obeyed their orders and started to disarm the Indians. At this, one of the holy men of the Miniconjou, Yellow Bird, put on his Ghost shirt and began to dance and sing. Tension rose. A young brave, Black Coyote, refused to give up his rifle. A shot rang out. Immediately the cavalrymen opened fire. The Sioux fought back with what weapons they had. Then they fled.

Source 2

The Ghost Dance. This photograph of the Arapaho tribe was taken in 1893.

The army fired Hotchkiss cannon (small mobile field cannon) at the backs of the fleeing Indians. Shells burst among them, tearing braves, squaws and children to pieces. It was all over in ten minutes.

Source 3

Marie Not Help Him remembers what she was told about the Battle of Wounded Knee. She is the great-great-granddaughter of Dewey Beard, who survived both the battle of Little Big Horn and the Battle of Wounded Knee.

Grandpa Beard said it was as if a huge canvas was being torn. The sound of the guns and the sound of the bullets hitting people, the screams, the horses being hit, and the commands of the soldiers. And seeing the women falling, the men falling. The shells would explode and pick up the children and throw them – it was like they were being tripped.

Source 4

Quoted in J. Neihardt, *Black Elk Speaks*, 1979.

Dead and wounded women and children and little babies were scattered all along there where they had been trying to run away. I saw a little baby trying to suck its mother, but she was bloody and dead.

Source 5

Quoted in *The Wild West*, Channel 4.

'Afterwards,' Private Jesse Harris said, 'I heard remarks from the older soldiers. "This is where we got even for the Battle of Little Big Horn." '

Source 6

Big Foot lying dead – and frozen in the snow – on the Wounded Knee battlefield. It wasn't until 3 January 1891 that the army finally collected the bodies of the 250 dead Indians. 146 were buried in a mass grave. About 50 Sioux survived.

The Nez Perce, the northern Cheyenne and the Apaches

The other tribes fared no better than the Sioux. For example, Chief Joseph and the Nez Perce from the north-western mountains resisted for a while, but in the end they were forced to go to Indian Territory (now Oklahoma). Dull Knife, Little Wolf and the northern Cheyenne also lost heart and were sent to Red Cloud's Pine Ridge Reservation. Geronimo led the Apaches in a fight against the US army from 1881–86, but they, too, surrendered in the end. Chief Joseph probably spoke for them all when he said:

Source 7

Chief Joseph of the Nez Perce. Quoted in Dee Brown, *Bury my Heart at Wounded Knee*, 1971.

I am tired of fighting. Our chiefs are killed. The old men are all dead. I am tired; my heart is sick and sad. From where the sun now stands I will fight no more for ever.

Questions

1   Read this song, which is called The Ghost Dancers' song. It was sung by the Indians as they danced. Here it has been translated into English.

Father, have pity on us
We are crying for thirst
All is gone!
We have nothing to eat
Father, we are poor.
We are very poor.
The buffalo are gone
They are all gone.
Take pity on us, Father,
We are dancing as you wished
Because you commanded us.
We dance hard,
We dance long –
Have pity,
Father, help us
You are close by in the dark
Hear us and help us.
Take away the white men
Send back the buffalo
We are poor and weak
We can do nothing alone
Help us to be what we once were –
Happy hunters of buffalo.

Does this source, by itself, explain why the US government was so afraid of the Ghost Dance? Explain your answer carefully.

2   The Indians won the Battle of Little Big Horn. Why were they not able to follow this with further victories?

The end of the struggle for the Great Plains

The white man had finally won the struggle for the Great Plains. The Indians had been cleared from their hunting grounds. There was now nothing to stop white people from claiming and settling all the land. They could now put it to the plough, grow crops and use the land as they believed it should be used. The US government, however, had to be certain that the Indians would stay on their reservations or remain in Indian Territory.

The end of Indian tribal life

The US government believed that they had to break Indian tribal bonds if they were to have any hope of persuading the Indians to live like white people. Indians were already being sent to schools to learn to read and write, and to learn about the white way of life. But there was always the chance their old tribal loyalties would surface if there were any problems to be faced.

In 1871 the US government decided that no more treaties should be signed with tribal chiefs. In the early 1880s it set up special councils amongst the tribes. These councils were to take over the powers which the government had earlier given to the chiefs to enable them look after their people on the reservations. In 1883 special courts took over the chiefs' powers to judge and to punish the Indians. In 1885, however, these courts were abolished. In future, the US federal law courts would keep law and order amongst the Indians on their reservations and punish any wrongdoers. The Indians had lost all their ability to govern themselves.

Source 1

A Kiowa Indian, Wohaw, painted this picture called 'The Red Man's Dilemma'. The Indian has turned away from the buffalo and the Great Plains, and is looking toward the cow and the ploughed farmland.

The Dawes Act, 1887

Many white Americans believed that, if Indians were ever to live like white people, they had to have land of their own to farm. The Dawes Act divided up the Indian reservations into farms of 160 acres for each adult and 80 acres for each child in an Indian family. The rest of the land on reservations was to be opened up to white settlers. However, the problem was that many Indians would not accept the land. Many of those who did sold it back to white men as soon as they could, for pitifully small amounts of money. Few Indians would agree that the land problem had been solved. Unhappy with the land which they had to farm, or landless because they had sold their plot to the first white bidder; without the security of their tribal band and their culture, the Indians became more and more dependent on white people to feed them and give them shelter. The reservations had gone, divided between Indians and whites who were prepared to farm the land. What, now, would happen to the Indian Territory?

The Oklahoma land race

On 23 March 1889 President Harrison announced that 2 million acres in Indian Territory would soon be opened to settlers. This land, the Cherokee outlet and the Oklahoma District, had been bought from the Creeks and Seminoles for around $4 million. Hundreds of illegal settlers, called 'Boomers', had moved on to Indian lands during the 1880s, but federal troops had always thrown them out. Railway companies also pressed the government to open up the Indian Territory. Finally, it was to be theirs. The land would be opened on 22 April 1889. Thousands of hopeful settlers gathered on the edge of the unopened territory a few days before this. At noon on 22 April, bugles, guns and flags told them they could cross the boundary. Across they rushed, hundreds of them, on horseback and in wagons. By sunset, tent cities stretched along the horizon. By 1905 the Dawes Act was extended into all Indian Territory; whites and Indians were to live in a similar way, and Indian Territory was no more.

Source 2

'The run' painted by John Noble shows the dash for land in Oklahoma, 2 April 1889.

Unit 8 Review

Questions

1   Look at the map on page 99 which shows the lands of the Plains Indians in 1865. Now look at the map on page 106, which shows the Indian reservations in 1875.
What happened in the ten years between 1865 and 1875 to explain the differences in the lands the Indians held?

2   How did the US government defeat the Indians? Copy the grid below. Fill it in, using the information in this chapter.

Event	What happened	Outcome
Fort Laramie Treaty, 1851		
Gold in Colorado, 1859		
Sand Creek massacre, 1864		
Bluff Creek, 1865		
Fetterman's trap, 1866		
Medicine Lodge Creek meeting, 1867		
Fort Laramie Treaty, 1868		
Battle of the River Washita, 1868		
Rosebud River, 1876		
Battle of Little Big Horn, 1876		
Battle of Wounded Knee, 1890		
Dawes Act, 1887		

3   Use the information and sources in this unit to explain whether or not you agree with what Dee Brown is saying here.

Dee Brown, Bury my Heart at Wounded Knee, 1971.

To justify these breaches of the 'permanent frontier', the policy makers in Washington invented 'Manifest destiny'. The Europeans and their descendants were ordained by destiny to rule all of America. They were the dominant race, and therefore responsible for the Indians – along with their lands, their forests and their mineral wealth.

Unit 9 · Epilogue

The desire of the Indians to follow their own way of life didn't end with the Dawes Act of 1887 or the Oklahoma land race. In March 1985 the US Supreme Court decided that the Oneida Indians, who had their lands in the eastern states taken away in the late eighteenth century, should have them back. Ten years later, in 1995, a group of Indians went to Glasgow to ask for the return of a Ghost Dance shirt worn at the Battle of Wounded Knee.

Source 1

This is the Ghost Dance shirt worn at the Battle of Wounded Knee, and which is now in the Kelvingrove Art Gallery and Museum, Glasgow, Scotland.

Native Americans discuss return of relic with council officials

By **DUNCAN BLACK**

NATIVE Americans yesterday began face-to-face negotiations with Glasgow museum officials for the return of a sacred Ghost shirt removed from the body of one of the victims of the Wounded Knee massacre.

The garment was taken from the body of a member of the Lakota Sioux after the US Army slaughtered more than 200 men, women, and children at Wounded Knee in December 1890.

The victims had been gathering for a Ghost Dance, a ritual to bring back the spirits of their ancestors, the vanished buffalo, and their traditional way of life.

The shirt came to Glasgow a couple of years after the massacre when it was sold by an interpreter travelling with Buffalo Bill's Wild West Show.

At first exclusively revealed in The Herald, members of the Wounded Knee Survivors' Association began a campaign for the return of the shirt after it was spotted at an exhibition by a Native American visiting Glasgow in 1992.

Letters have gone back and forth since then but now the association has sent delegates to Scotland. Yesterday, they held talks with officials from Glasgow District Council's department of museums and art galleries at Kelvingrove Art Gallery and Museum, where the Ghost Shirt is on display.

The talks covered not only the Ghost Shirt but also some other items, including ceremonial pipes, held by the museums department. Mr Gonzalez, delegation leader, said: "I feel that eventually we will arrive at an agreement where these items can be repatriated to the rightful owners.

"There are legal reasons why they should be returned but the ethical and moral reasons are the strongest."

Mr Mark O'Neill, the department's senior curator of history, described the meeting as "very moving and informative" and said the delegation had made a strong case for the return of the items.

However, he added: "We made the point that we have an obligation to educate our public about the history of the world through the objects we have in our collection. Our dilemma is to reconcile the rights we acknowledge that the Lakota have to these objects and our duties to our citizens."

The talks are continuing.

Source 2

Part of an article by Duncan Black published in the *Glasgow Herald (Herald)*, 11 April 1995.

Questions

1   In 1931 Charles Russell wrote in the book *Trails Plowed Under* that:

> The red man was the true American. They have almost all gone, but will never be forgotten. The history of how they fought for their country is written in blood, a stain that time cannot grind out.

Was he correct? Use what you know to support your opinion.

What happened on the Great Plains?

1840   1850   186

Indians

lived on the Great Plains

1840
U.S. government says that Great Plains are Indian Territory

1851
Fort Laramie Treaty (1)

Early Settlers

crossed the Great Plains

1840–50
55,000 arrive in California and Oregon by wagon train

1848–57
Miners courts and vigilantes

1846
Donner Party

1850
Peak year for migration

1847
Mormons reach the Great Salt Lake

1858–59
Gold discovered in the Rocky Mountains

1848
Gold discovered in California

Cattlemen and cowboys

worked on the Great Plains

Trails blazed from Texas to New Orleans, Ohio, Chicago, California

Homesteaders

lived and worked on the Great Plains

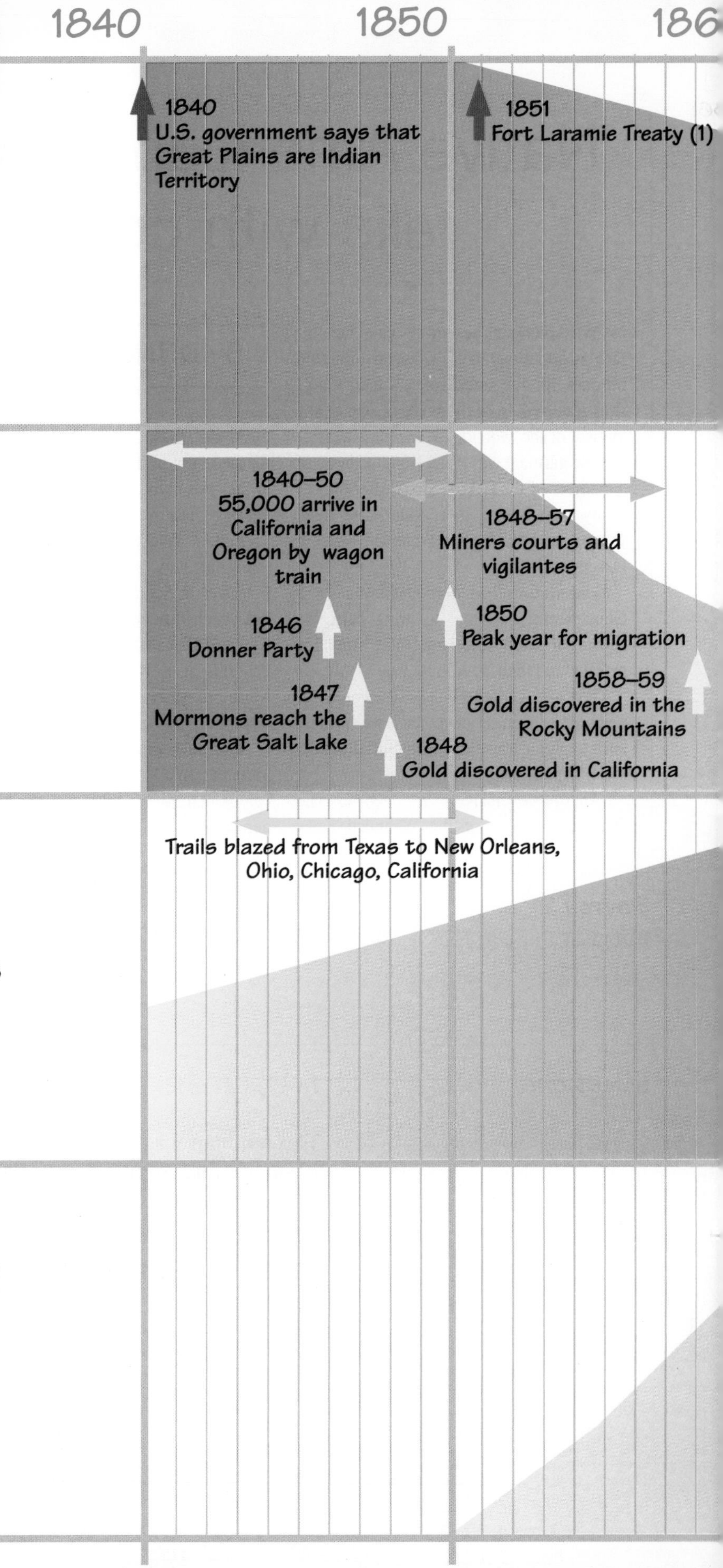

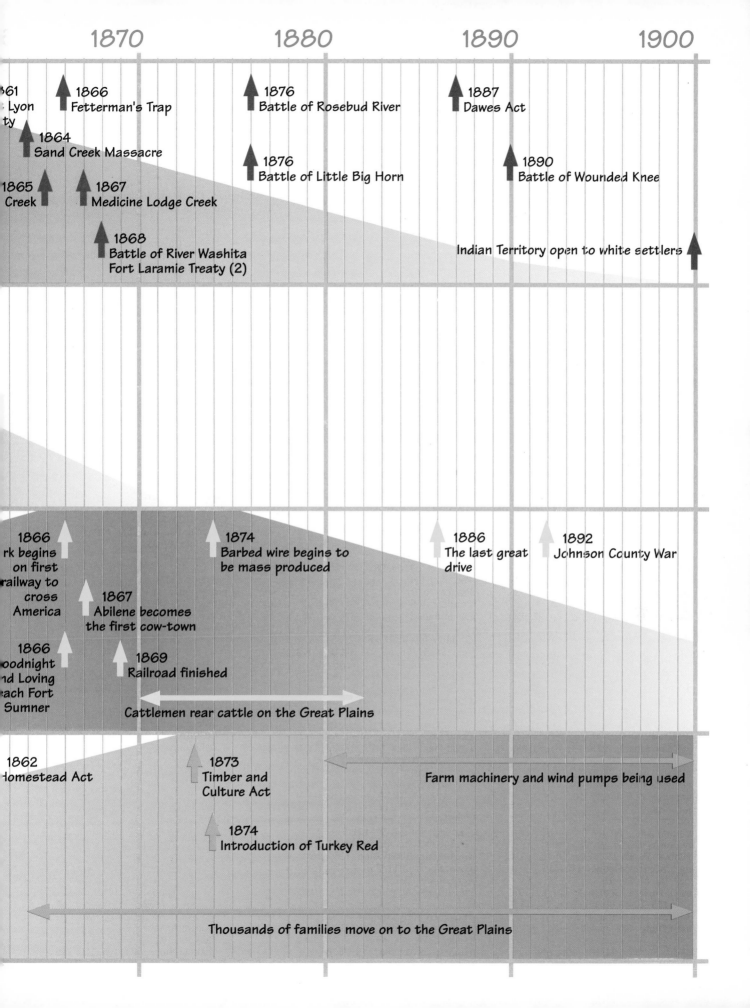

1870   1880   1890   1900

361
Lyon
ty

1866
Fetterman's Trap

1876
Battle of Rosebud River

1887
Dawes Act

1864
Sand Creek Massacre

1876
Battle of Little Big Horn

1890
Battle of Wounded Knee

1865
Creek

1867
Medicine Lodge Creek

1868
Battle of River Washita
Fort Laramie Treaty (2)

Indian Territory open to white settlers

1866
rk begins
on first
railway to
cross
America

1874
Barbed wire begins to
be mass produced

1886
The last great
drive

1892
Johnson County War

1867
Abilene becomes
the first cow-town

1866
oodnight
nd Loving
each Fort
Sumner

1869
Railroad finished

Cattlemen rear cattle on the Great Plains

1862
Homestead Act

1873
Timber and
Culture Act

Farm machinery and wind pumps being used

1874
Introduction of Turkey Red

Thousands of families move on to the Great Plains

Index